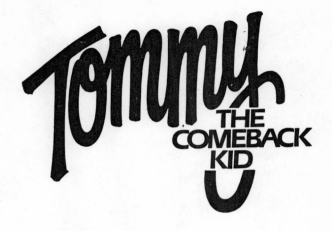

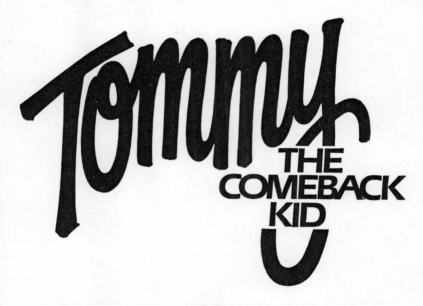

Thomas Fulghum

VICTOR

BOOKS a division of SP Publications, Inc.
WHEATON, ILLINOIS 60187

Offices also in
Whitby, Ontario, Canada
Amersham-on-the-Hill, Bucks, England

Cover photograph by Dan Lower

Scripture quotations are from the *King James Version* (KJV)
and *The Living Bible* (LB), © 1971, Tyndale House Publishers,
Wheaton, Illinois. Used by permission.

Recommended Dewey Decimal Classification: 248.4
   Suggested Subject Headings: Suffering; Courage

Library of Congress Catalog Card Number: 82-61705
ISBN: 0-88207-649-3

VICTOR BOOKS
A division of SP Publications, Inc.
P.O. Box 1825 • Wheaton, Illinois 60187

Contents

Dedication

To my son, Tom
The Comeback Kid
who never gave up or looked back.
His faith and courage are a constant inspiration to me.

To my wife, Lois
and to our children, Becky, Brian, Kevin, and Karen
who demonstrated a courage of their own.

Appreciation

To all those who stood with us in prayer,
helped us financially, and in other ways encouraged us,
especially the Christian community in our beloved Ecuador.

To Carole Streeter, who encouraged me to write this book,
and to Lois Reimer, who typed the manuscript.

Foreword

Tommy, a happy, healthy boy I met in Quito, Ecuador, became a teenager I later knew in Wheaton, Illinois: a young man slowly and painfully coming back from a devastating accident.

This book tells of his raw courage and determination.

But it is as much the story of his parents' courage, from the moment in the emergency room when Tom desperately examined that terribly damaged head to tell whether it was his son or not, to Lois's tears as her son walked across the platform to receive his high school diploma.

From my acquaintance with Becky, young Tom's sister, I know something of the struggles she and the rest of the family went through during Tom's recovery. Without doubt their patience and high expectations played a large part in this remarkable story.

I have a deep appreciation for this family and their Christian testimony. It would therefore be surprising if I didn't think this book was outstanding.

But as I read it, I am impressed with the book's excellence: the author's honesty; the way he avoids the trap of playing on our emotions; the simple, natural way he presents an overarching spiritual perspective. There is no doubt about the source of all that courage.

Thomas Fulghum was already a Christian communicator, through broadcasting at HCJB, and teaching. He has now proved that he can also communicate through writing.

—Joseph Bayly

1
The Accident

"What should I do?" I wondered. "Should I stand up and applaud? Or walk over and give Tom a big hug when he comes across the stage?" The tension in the gym continued to build as the moment approached. The graduate just before Tom was called and the applause rose and fell. "That's what I'll do! I'll get up and give him a big hug," I decided.

"Thomas David Fulghum," the principal called, as Tom stepped onto the platform. The applause rose as with all the others before him, but it continued to rise as he limped across the stage. Many of those present were aware of how much he had overcome to reach this point. "This is his moment," I mused, "and I must not get into it. He deserves to savor it all by himself."

I knew that Lois must be crying now. And my own eyes were filled with hot tears. The applause mounted as Tom reached out to take his diploma. Then, tassel turned, he limped smiling from the platform. It wa a brief moment, but it was his, jammed full of struggles and dreams, hopes and accomplishments.

The two days just prior to commencement had been awards days. Awards had been given for academic achievement and athletic prowess. But the awards that Tom deserved are not given at such events. Whoever heard of an award for learning to walk again? Or one for learning to talk again? There may be awards for mountain climbing, but there are no awards for climbing out of an abyss of human misery and debilitation. Now, as the tears coursed down my cheeks, in my heart I was pinning all those medals on him. And I was awarding him highest honors for academic achievement and blue ribbons for physical accomplishment, not to mention a huge trophy for his courage.

Years before, Tom had been near the top of his class and was destined to be a school leader. His brilliant mind was often discussed by his teachers and the future seemed incredibly bright. As his parents, Lois and I felt as if God had entrusted us with an angel and we were proud to bear that responsibility.

While we hurt for him now, as those traditional honors evaded him, we were more convinced than ever that God had allowed us to have a very special son whom He loved in some unusual way. Our pride at his graduation from high school could not be surpassed by any other awards he might receive. He had made it on his own. He had graduated with his class, and this was an accomplishment beyond description. No certificate or plaque could contain what that really meant.

No one else in the auditorium could really understand how deep were the depths from which he had ascended. Oh, many had seen him in the early hours and days after his accident and had watched and prayed as he crept slowly away from the edge of death. But only Lois and I had been continually by his side and had watched him claw his way back to life and to something more than raw existence.

How many times had we wished we could roll back the clock

and return to our comfortable lifestyle before his accident?. How many times had we wanted to give Tom the opportunity to grow up in some normal way? And how repeatedly had we longed that all the original promise and potential could be returned to him? How often had we wondered what we might have done differently that night? How many times had we visualized that horrible scene, on a night five-and-a-half years earlier?

o o o o o o

The rain beat softly on the streets of Quito, Ecuador as Tommy stepped out of the lighted doorway and into the night. He quickened his steps to the corner, his thoughts intent on the homework which awaited him.

He had decided not to stay for refreshments like the other kids in the band. He had paused by the food-laden tables long enough to gaze at the selection of cookies, cakes, and other goodies until his sense of duty urged him to stride out into the rainy night.

Pausing at the corner, he waited for the traffic light to blink to green, then stepped onto the Panamerican Highway to cross to the bus stop on the other side. He didn't hear the red sports car which sped out of the blackness, headlights dark and un-searching. It never occurred to him that anyone would consider running a red light, for that was against the law, and Tommy would never deliberately break the law.

But the car came, the driver sensing the surge of the engine beneath the hood. It gave him a feeling of power as he urged it through the abandoned streets. Surely, no one would be out walking on such a night. He turned off the headlights, search-ing for any shiny reflection on the wet pavement that would indicate the approach of a vehicle from the other direction.

There was none. Ignoring the red traffic light which seemed to serve no useful function on the deserted street, he pressed the accelerator to the floor and the car's engine responded with authority.

Suddenly, as if from nowhere, the figure of a young boy appeared through the rain-spattered windshield. In a moment of terror he tried to avoid the inevitable. He jammed on his brakes, but it was a useless exercise. The car careened on until he heard the sickening crash of the boy's body on the hood as the car spun wildly down the street. Finally, the screeching of the brakes ceased and the car came to a stop. Only the quiet patter of the soft rain continued. The street seemed deserted. No one came running to the scene of the crash. No one had seen the young boy's body fly through the air, then tumble to a stop in the dark street.

Gripped by terror, the driver jammed the car into gear, spun around wildly, and sped off into the night, leaving Tommy to die.

o o o o o o

I was feeling great about the way my evening was going. A Latin American radio network of Christian ministry, which encompassed South and Central America, was airing a series of satellite broadcasts of the Luis Palau Managua Crusade—a first of its kind. This was the opening night. I was involved with missionary radio station HCJB, which served as the base station for 55 other radio outlets that would repeat our signal throughout the Spanish-speaking world. Millions would hear the Gospel through this month-long effort.

I felt good because the English program I just finished went smoothly and according to plan. It was interesting and fun to have as our guest the director of the Costa Rican Symphony

Orchestra. He was an American who had grown up in Douglas, Arizona. His high school was the rival my high school played in the Turkey Day football game every year at Thanksgiving time. Though Douglas High School was considerably bigger than the one I attended in Bisbee, there was never any doubt in my mind about which one was the best. And now I was meeting a former foe so far south in Quito, Ecuador. The program went well as we talked about how two Arizona boys got to Latin America, and reminisced on the air about the old days.

Humming happily to myself, I hurried from one radio studio to another, anxious to be briefed on the progress of the satellite network. "How are things going, Ken?" I asked Ken Grant, who was handling the audio controls and the satellite line to HCJB's expanded audience.

"Well, the network transmission is going just great. However ... well, I hope it was OK, but I gave permission for an announcement to be made over our FM station in Spanish and in English."

"I'm sure it's OK, Ken," I responded curiously, "but what was the nature of the announcement?" I was puzzled because we rarely make announcements on our FM station except for special reasons.

"Well, there is a husky blond kid over in our emergency room and no one can identify him. He was hit on the Panamerican Highway over two hours ago. We thought that perhaps some parent might be wondering why his child hasn't come home and hear the announcement on the radio. We've been hoping for someone to give us a call."

Immediately I thought about my own family. The kids were playing in the band for a parent-teacher meeting that night. I quickly went to my office and phoned home.

"Honey, are the children home?" I asked my wife, Lois.

"Becky and Chuck are here, but I can't imagine where Tommy is," she responded. "When he didn't come home with them, I just assumed he was with you." Becky, our oldest daughter, and Chuck, our nephew, had remained for refreshments and had been given a ride. It was unusual for Tommy to be the last one home.

"Honey, I'm afraid I have an idea of where he might be, but I don't like it. There is a husky blond boy in our hospital who has been hit by a car. It sounds bad. No one has been able to identify him."

"Oh, no . . . !" Lois shuddered.

"What was Tommy wearing when he left home?" I queried.

"He was wearing his jeans and striped shirt. He also had his new jean jacket," she answered.

I felt sick to my stomach as I crossed the street from the radio station to the hospital. Entering by the main door, I was met by a host of inquirers, all wondering who the poor boy could be. Many had tried to identify him, but without success.

"Tom, could you help us out?" inquired school principal, Bob Trempert. His brow was furrowed by deep concern. "We have this boy here who was . . ."

"I know," I interrupted. "Ken told me about it. Bob, Tommy didn't come home after the program tonight."

"Tommy!" he gasped. "But we all know Tommy, and it doesn't look like . . ." He stopped abruptly. "Well, you had better take a look."

My heart pounding, I entered the emergency room to find the heaving frame of a boy stripped and partly covered with a sheet. His bare chest rose and fell in a grotesque and rapid beat. A large white plastic tube protruded from his mouth. His head was tremendously enlarged and his eyes looked like two huge purple balls. He was in terrible trouble.

I walked around the table, straining to discern the likeness of a familiar face. Then walking back the other way, I moved to the other side of the table. I dropped to my knees beside the cot on which he lay, trying to get another perspective of the side which seemed less swollen, but I could not recognize any likeness to my son. "May I see his clothing?" I asked. "It's impossible to tell by looking at him." I was hoping beyond hope that I would not see any recognizable garment.

Two nurses scurried to gather the clothes which had been cut from his body. As they entered the room, my eyes fell immediately on the belt which one of them carried. It was Tommy's belt. My spirits plummeted to despair.

"It's . . . I'm afraid . . . I'm sorry to say . . ." My being sought to reject what I knew to be the truth. "This is my son. It's Tommy. I can't believe this is happening, but . . . it . . . it is . . . our Tom."

"O God . . . No!" rasped Dr. Cesar Cabascango. Then quickly recovering his professional demeanor, he spoke in measured tones. "Tom, your boy has suffered multiple fractures of both legs, multiple fractures of the arms, multiple fractures of the pelvis, and multiple fractures of the skull. He may have other injuries of which we are not aware, but I need your signature on a release form, as we may have to do surgery. Tom, the prognosis is very poor. Should surgery be necessary, I doubt that he can make it."

I already knew his prognosis was grim. That was readily apparent. I looked at the boy on the table. "No, dear God, that can't be Tommy. It doesn't look at all like him," I protested. Then looking at the belt in my hand, I inwardly despaired, "Yes, it has to be Tommy. This is his belt." I went back and forth between disbelief and admission several times, trying desperately to extricate us from the dilemma we were in. But I could not.

Suddenly, in the midst of the despair, the Lord interrupted

my thinking and spoke to me. "Tom," He said, "in everything give thanks, for this is the will of God concerning you."

"Give thanks?" I argued. "What in the world for?" The whole idea seemed inappropriate, irrelevant, and absurd. But again the Lord spoke to me and strongly urged, "In everything give thanks, for this is the will of God concerning you" (1 Thessalonians 5:18).

Peering through my tears, I turned and walked to the corner of the room. With parched lips I began to express the thanks that my heart did not feel. It was simply a prayer of obedience, not an expression of great spiritual victory. I did what I knew I had to, not what I felt like doing.

I hardly knew how to begin, but as I did, the Lord began to lead me in my praying. "Lord, I thank You that You are the sovereign God, the King of kings and the Lord of lords. I thank You that You are absolutely perfect. You never make a mistake in what You do or in what You allow. I thank You that You are omnipotent. There is nothing too hard for You to do. I thank You that You are omniscient. You see the end from the beginning and there is nothing hidden from Your eyes and understanding. I thank You that You give wisdom to those who ask for it. I thank You that You are love and that perfect love casts out fear. You love Tommy. You love Lois and me, and You love our family. And Lord, I thank You that You are immutable and that though heaven and earth may pass away, You remain constant and eternal. Everything in this life may change, but You never change. I thank You too, Lord, for Your faithfulness. You are the One in whom we can really put our trust."

At the time I prayed that prayer, I didn't realize what the Holy Spirit of God was doing. He was leading me to recognize the attributes of God, because it would be upon those very attributes that all our hopes and all our trust would come to rest. Somehow, in my agony, and in the midst of tremendous confusion and apparent disaster, I knew that all of the things that I had prayed were exactly true. This was the God we had known and served, and He had not changed.

I turned, dried my tears, and went to find Lois who had arrived at the hospital.

2
Intensive Care

Standing without speaking, Lois and I looked at the battered body of our son. He lay in a maze of hoses, wires, and tubes. The large plastic apparatus was still protruding from his mouth and went down his gullet to prevent the swelling of his face and throat from cutting off his air supply. His husky chest rose and fell tempestuously. The beeper on the heart monitor frantically announced the terrible plight he was in.

"Can a heart really beat that fast, that irregularly, and keep going?" I wondered. "How long can he endure such hard and labored breathing? Can he hold together under such an incredible pace?" It did not seem possible. It seemed that he would soon be torn apart by the assault on his body by systems that were out of control.

As I looked at him lying there, I thought about what a good kid he was. He was Mr. Obedience in our family. He was happy, positive, and dependable. If we really wanted something done, we gave it to Tommy and he always did his best. He continually offered his help, and if he ever resented being called upon so frequently, he never showed it. There was no spirit of rebellion in him, and his sweet Christian spirit was noticed by everyone. And now as I looked at his pathetic body, my tears wanted to flow, but couldn't. I felt like they were dammed up behind the lump which throbbed in the back of my throat.

It was then that I first felt it. It started in the pit of my stomach and began to work its way up through my body. It began as a smouldering ash, but as the moments passed, it grew into an angry flame as if fanned by the winds of Tommy's rapid breath.

As Lois gently stroked Tommy's brow and ran her fingers through his hair, only her eyes revealed the pain she was bearing. She was quiet, but that was characteristic of Lois. She has always suffered in silence, like when she gave birth to Tommy. I had been with her at the birth of two of our children, and she never cried out when she hurt. Her quiet suffering had somehow been an encouragement to me. It was now.

But the anger continued to rise in my soul. How could a man run down an unsuspecting child and leave him to die in the rainy night? What kind of creature could turn his back on a boy in the throes of a deep peril, a peril that he himself had created?

Beads of perspiration began to form on my forehead as molten rage surged through my veins. I wanted to hit somebody or kick something. I wanted to cry. But I did neither. I just stood there looking at Tommy.

Then God spoke to me again, as He had in the emergency room. It must have been the same voice that calmed the storm on the Sea of Galilee. It felt like a gentle breeze blowing away the storm that raged inside me so that I could listen. I heard His quiet voice say to me, "Tom, would you consider allowing Tommy to go through this for a friend?"

"No way!" I objected. "I would never willingly let him go through this for anyone. I might be willing to do it myself, but not him . . . not anything like this."

"Then would you consider sending him to go through some-thing like this for an enemy?" That question was more shock-ing than the first one, but immediately the point of what He was saying was clear. What a stern rebuke to my anger! I was overwhelmed.

The Lord was sending me a message which was awesome. For the first time in my life, I was learning to comprehend, at least in some measure, the extent of God's love. He had volun-tarily sacrificed His Son, and Jesus had willingly been beaten beyond recognition for my sin. Tom never knew what hit him, but Jesus had been abused, mocked, and tortured over many hours by a godless mob, and He suffered out of love for me, the one who caused His pain. And because of Christ's sacrifice I had received a complete pardon. How could I, who had experi-enced total forgiveness at such a price, not forgive the one who had committed this sin against my boy?

"O God, please forgive my hateful heart, and thank You for showing me how deep Your forgiveness can reach. Lord, I forgive the one who hit Tommy, whoever he is. And I pray for him, that he too might experience Your forgiveness just as I have. I pray that instead of carrying an incredible guilt all of his life for what he did tonight, he might experience Your peace. I pray that at this moment, while he must be agonizing over what has happened, he will cry out to You and that when he calls, You will answer and meet his need."

As surely as the anger had risen in my heart, it began to disappear in the same way. The hateful thoughts changed to pity. The anger which burned melted into compassion for the pitiable soul who would probably relive that awful moment 1,000 times. I actually wanted to cry for him.

God in His mercy had recognized the peril I was in, and was preventing me from being consumed by a bitterness that could have taken a toll on me for the rest of my life. I never again felt hatred for the stranger whose carelessness had forever altered our lives. The Lord had spared me from the crippling disease of unforgiveness and bitterness.

I later witnessed such bitterness in the lives of many others who had suffered. They carried deep within them resentments and angers which gnawed continuously at their existence. As long as the unforgiveness remained, they would never have peace of mind or heart, nor would full faith in the Lord blossom. Some never expressed their bitterness toward the Lord. Yet underneath, the emaciated remains of a faith they could not recover continued to decay. They did not realize that God brings only good things into our lives. He cannot be the author of evil. Even in what He allows, He has an ultimate plan which is for our good.

We must take the first steps of forgiveness, because God taught us how. But we cannot completely forgive until, by an act of our wills, we purpose to do so. And then by His spirit, He provides what is needed in grace to perfect that forgiveness.

Sitting by Tommy's side, we wondered if perhaps he could hear us. We remembered the stories of others who had been in a comatose state. They later recounted that they had heard every word spoken in their presence. They were locked inside their injured bodies, unable to speak, though they had desperately wanted to do so. Sometimes it seemed to us that Tommy could faintly squeeze our hands when we asked him to do so. Surely if he could hear, he knew the grim evaluation of his condition. What would be in his mind? What fears were trapped inside his body?

Privately, Lois and I agreed to speak only that which was good, comforting, and encouraging while in his presence. We would not mention the darker possibilities, nor would we allow others to do so. We would major on the hopeful and positive progress which he made.

Then it occurred to us that Tommy might like to have us sing to him. He loved the choruses and songs we sang at our home prayer meetings and in our little Spanish church. In Spanish we sang Psalm 34 which was one of his favorites.

I will bless the Lord at all times.
His praise shall continually be in my mouth.
My soul shall make her boast in the Lord.
The humble shall hear it and rejoice.
Oh magnify the Lord with me.
And let us exalt His name together.
I sought the Lord and He heard me
and delivered me from all my fears.

We were often unaware of the Ecuadorian nurses and aides who stood near the door watching. Many of those girls didn't know the Lord. They must have wondered how we could sing those words at a time when our oldest son lay in the trauma of silent anguish. Given the same circumstances in some of the other hospital cases, those nurses were accustomed to crying and wailing, not singing. They expected hysteria, not tranquility.

It was a wonder to us too, but the songs ministered to us as we sang them. They reminded us that God was in control and that He loves us all. He was doing the thing which He alone does so well: attending to our needs and, at the same time, meeting the needs of others around us. That is so like the Lord. He never said that we would be free from tribulation in this world, but He promised that during our tribulations and trials He would be there with us. He promised never to leave us. Often He seems nearest when the trials are most grievous. So it was with us. It was not that we were superspiritual people. It was a matter of having great need, and because He was there meeting that need, we could sing.

I tried to come to grips with the reality that my son was

between life and death, but the Lord knew I needed to change my perspective on that subject. Each time I began thinking "life and death," the Lord would interrupt my thoughts and interject "life and life everlasting." What a difference in perspective that was! For the unbeliever, between life and death is indeed the most perilous place to be. But for the child of God, between life and life everlasting is not a bad place to be at all. That is why the Apostle Paul struggled with the issue when he longed to be with Christ which was, as he said, far better. Yet he longed to remain in this life as well, if it were in God's best interest and in the best interests of the church. Why do we cling to life? Is it because we desire to serve God and our fellowmen, or is it simply for selfish reasons?

When I think about the rise in teenage suicides, I grow concerned, because it is not normal for a person to want to die, not even for the child of God. In Tommy's case, he was not a rebellious or wayward boy. He loved life and he loved to live it with others. He found great joy in pleasing the Lord, his parents, and his friends.

But he was now between life and life everlasting rather than life and death, not because of his goodness but because he had a great personal relationship with God. Even though he was only in seventh grade, Tommy faithfully read his Bible. Often Lois would enter his room at night and remove the Bible from his chest where it had fallen when he had drifted off to sleep while reading it. He loved the Lord, and the Lord loved him, and we knew that. What a tremendous comfort that was to us in those moments.

When we had to leave the Intensive Care Unit, we'd go out into the hall where many of our HCJB family and friends waited with us. If we had to choose one good place in the world to suffer tragedy, it would be there. The HCJB family and the larger missionary community were close around us to uphold and help us in scores of ways. Some of those very people had passed through similar crises and understood how we felt. Some of our friends chatted quietly with us and sought to bring comfort. Others just sat and prayed silently, but they didn't need to say anything. Their quiet support was sometimes even more encouraging than the more verbal kind. Many went home and prayed because of the crowded conditions in the hospital. Tommy's entire school sought the Lord on his behalf. The gates of heaven were being stormed by the petitions of the saints.

During one of my vigils in the hall, a friend approached me and whispered, "The Lord must love you a great deal to trust you with something like this." At first the very thought almost angered me. The whole idea seemed like an absurdity. I really wanted to dismiss that notion, but I could not. How could such a thing as this terrible accident be interpreted as a loving act? It haunted my conscious mind for many weeks and months, and became a sort of riddle that demanded a resolution.

On one occasion, I began to ask myself why this terrible thing had happened to us. But almost as quickly as I raised the question, I realized that I could get into a long and meaningless debate with myself searching for the answer. The question did have an answer, but it was known only to God at that point. We would have to wait to learn the lesson God had in mind from this experience. I prayed earnestly that we would learn every lesson there was. We were paying too high a price not to profit from it in some way.

The long night crept by. Minutes turned to hours, and the hours into what seemed an eternity. The heart monitor beeped wildly through the night. Tommy's chest rose and fell like the waves of an angry sea. We waited and prayed. There was nothing else to do.

At 3 A.M., Dr. Wally Swanson emerged from Tommy's room.

His face was grave as he beckoned us to enter. We quickly responded. As we did, Wally gathered us into his arms. He was a good man, a compassionate doctor, and a friend. He had not left Tommy's side since his arrival at the hospital.

"Tom and Lois," he said softly with pain in his voice, "I'm so sorry, but your boy isn't doing very well. His heartbeat is out of control. His breathing, though fast, is shallow, and his blood pressure is not good. He has put up a good fight. He is a strong boy." We looked at our boy on the bed. Life seemed to be slipping away from him.

Again the Lord began to speak to me. He reminded me that when Tommy was born we had made a commitment to Him. As Lois and I held him for the first time, admiring our little red package with the strawberry blond hair, we had bowed in prayer and thanked the Lord for this gift of young life, and we had promised to raise him in the love of God. "He is Yours, dear Lord," we had said, "and You have given him to us to care for and to love. We want to be good guardians of this trust." We looked at the little person who blinked in wonder at these strangers who held him in their arms. He was so cute. His hair started far back on his head which gave him a sort of middle-aged hairline. We used to say that he looked like his Uncle Willie, who had a hairline identical to his.

And now we thought about the promise we had made 12 years ago. "Well, Honey," I sighed, "we committed him to the Lord for His own purposes and I guess He needs him in heaven."

Laying my hand on his bare foot I prayed, "Dear Lord, I want to thank You again for giving Tommy to us for these 12 wonderful years. He has been a special son. You know, Lord, that when he was born, we gave him back to You for You to do Your will with his life. Therefore, if it is Your choice to take him to Yourself, then we release him into Your care. He is not ours to hold. Heaven will be richer because he is there. But Lord, as

Tommy's mom and dad, we would love to keep him here, if that could be a part of Your plan. Please work out Your divine purpose in him, and in us."

Dr. Wally and the nurses continued to work over him as we stepped back out into the hall. Our friends looked at us with compassion sensing that the situation was even more desperate than before. The we heard it. The buzzer on the breathing machine, that sounds when a patient ceases to respond to it, began to wail. We stared at each other teary eyed. "He's gone," I said huskily as I took Lois into my arms. Holding each other tightly, we prayed again and thanked the Lord that He had been in complete control.

Lois smiled sadly and whispered, "I guess we will never have Esther as a daughter-in-law." It was a curious thing to say, but it somehow seemed appropriate because it addressed itself to our hopes and aspirations for Tommy and for his future. I had often teased Tommy about a little freckled-faced girl in his class who I thought was special. And though no one ever took seriously any romantic ideas for Tommy and Esther, it was an expression of desire that Tommy would grow up and meet a young lady who was special in the same sense. We would not have to concern ourselves with those kinds of ideas any longer.

Amazingly, we did not grieve. We sensed an enormous peace, for the presence of God was with us in that place. It was a beautiful reminder that we who know the Lord do not grieve as those who have no hope. We had full knowledge that Tommy knew the Lord, and that to be absent from his body meant being present with the Lord. We would join him someday in the presence of Jesus. (See 1 Thessalonians 4:13 and 2 Corinthians 5:8.)

When death occurs in Ecuador, it is customary to have the burial service the next day. Suddenly we were aware of the many arrangements which needed to be taken care of quickly.

We had already begun to discuss our son's funeral plans, asking ourselves who should preside and who should be the ones involved in other ways in his funeral, when the door to the intensive care unit opened and Dr. Wally emerged. He looked peaceful enough about things.

"Well, he's doing a little better," he declared. He was obviously pleased.

We were confused. What did he mean by that? In my bewilderment, I stammered, "I'm afraid I don't understand, isn't he. . . . I mean, didn't he . . . You mean he is still alive?"

"Yes!" Wally responded. "He seemed to be fighting the respirator, so we took it off, and he's doing a little better on his own. His breathing is less shallow and his blood pressure has increased substantially."

What did this mean? Would the Lord give us back our son, or was it just a matter of more time before He would take him? We didn't dare form any opinions on that question. We could only wait and see what would take place.

The wait grew deeper and longer as Tommy labored through the night in his quest to survive. What an encouragement it was to us each time we looked at the HCJB staff members and friends who sat silently by. What a privilege it had been to serve on the staff with such marvelous people. And how Tommy loved them. He was completely happy in Ecuador and felt that these individuals were his own aunts and uncles.

"The Lord must love you a great deal to trust you with something like this!" That statement kept coming back to me, and I kept rejecting it. It just didn't make any sense to me. Could this tragedy possibly be motivated by the love of God? I could accept His sovereign control over the situation, but it seemed like more a matter of His permissive will and government than of His love.

"If he makes it through the first 24 hours, it will be a good sign," the doctor said. Immediately we began to calculate the hours, and the countdown began. I never dreamed that time could move so slowly. It was as if all time had come to a complete stop—as if we had been put on hold. It always seemed to be T-minus something and holding. But the time finally did pass, and when it did, it was extended to 48 hours and then later to 72. Though the hours passed and turned into days, Tommy's physical condition remained almost unchanged.

On the first morning after the accident, a neighbor from our apartment house slipped a note into our hands. She said, "I hope this will encourage you. It's a promise that the Lord gave as I was praying for Tommy last night." We opened the note and read the psalm which was written there:

For the Lord says, "Because he loves Me, I will rescue him;
I will make him great because he trusts in My name.
When he calls on Me I will answer;
I will be with him in trouble, and rescue him and honor him.
I will satisfy him with a full life
and give him My salvation" (Psalm 91:14–16, LB).

That promise from God's Word would prove to be a great source of comfort and encouragement to us for many months to come. It was impossible to imagine how God would rescue Tommy—or us—but we desperately clung to that promise and to the Lord. It seemed that each hour brought a new crisis. One such dilemma forced us to make a fast decision as to whether we'd permit the doctors to do an angiogram. This test would determine whether brain surgery would be necessary to relieve the pressures that were building there. The exam itself was very dangerous and could be fatal. But not to do it could even be worse if there were internal bleeding. We agreed to the test and waited. Tommy came through the test without incident, and the results showed there was no need for surgery. We praised the Lord.

On the third day, a different crisis arose. Body temperature is controlled by the brain, and Tommy's entire brain function had gone haywire. His temperature began to soar. Higher and higher it climbed as nurses and aides bathed his body with alcohol, but to no avail.

"Oh, if we only had one of those thermobeds," one of the nurses said. "If we don't get this temperature under control, it will either kill him or do severe damage to his brain."

"What's a thermobed?" I inquired.

"It's a mattress that is commonly used in U.S. hospitals to regulate body temperature. It works by flooding the body with warm or cool water."

In minutes I was on the prowl for an air mattress. Within a half an hour we were pouring ice water into one from a pitcher through a funnel. Thirty minutes later, Tommy's fever began to recede. We praised the Lord again.

Tommy lay on the water mattress for many weeks. It helped not only in controlling his temperature but also in preventing bedsores.

During those early days after the accident, HCJB missionaries Leonard and Imogene Booker offered to exchange houses with us. They lived across from the hospital and thought it would be easier for us to be closer to Tommy.

Years earlier, before we had met the Bookers, HCJB President Abe VanDerPuy had described them to us as anchor people. And now they helped to anchor us by their love, understanding, and prayer, during the long hours and days.

3
Home for the Holidays

The days turned into weeks, and with the passing of time, Tommy's heartbeat, temperature, and breathing began to stabilize. By the fourth day, we had slight but guarded glimpses of optimism for his survival. But the vigils continued. Different friends from HCJB and other missions took turns sitting with him through the long nights. It was a frightening experience. Tommy's breathing had been too fast in the earlier days, but now it was very shallow and slow. Many times he would take two deep breaths and then would not breathe again for 10 to 13 seconds. This seemed like an eternity. Sometimes after a big sigh, he would not breathe for even a longer time, and every time he did that, the individual who was with him was sure he had died.

We continued to sit by his bed and talk to him or sing to him in the hope that he might be encouraged. He continued in his silent sleep. On rare occasions, I could feel his hand slightly squeeze mine. Was he inside his body somewhere trying to get out, but unable to do so? Could he hear and understand, but not respond? If so, was he afraid? We felt we needed to express only love and encouragement to him, so we never stopped speaking to him in those terms.

During this period of constant watching and waiting, our appreciation for what it means to be a part of God's family expanded beyond the boundaries of our understanding.

The beauty of the kingdom of God unfolded to us as multiple expressions of love and concern enveloped us like rivers of healing water. We were buoyed up and showered in a warm torrent of continuous affection which was demonstrated in too many ways to number.

Soft words, gentle smiles, warm meals, and helping hands were the ever-present elements of this beautiful family support. We often struggled with how to express our gratitude to these many Christian brothers and sisters who were so important to us at that moment. "Thank you" seemed too inadequate to express what was in our hearts, and yet it was the best that human language could provide. I guess it's the same way when we try to express to the Lord what we really want to say to Him, but at least we know that the Holy Spirit is expressing what we feel.

What a blessing they were to us as we saw them sitting with Tommy throughout the night hours and ministering to our family in so many other ways. When they sat with him at night, they took the risk that something could happen during their watch which would be frightening or difficult to handle, but they were still willing to run that risk in order that we might get the rest we needed and that Tommy would have the watch-care which was necessary.

It had been three weeks since the accident and the neurosurgeon felt that the time had come to measure the extent of damage done to Tommy's brain. He entered his room with numerous instruments and closed the door. Lois and I stood tensely by outside and waited, hoping for a good result. How long it really took the doctor I couldn't say, but after what seemed like forever he emerged from Tommy's room shaking his head from side to side. Then with a dark look and furrowed brow he muttered, "The damage is very serious . . . very serious. I'm sorry." With that, he made his way down the hall, still shaking his head. He was very dismayed by the results.

But what did that mean? We really didn't know. We knew it was not good news, but we still didn't understand what it meant in Tommy's situation. We later learned that no one else really knew what it meant either. One neurosurgeon said that trying to discern information about the brain is like trying to listen to a single conversation in a stadium teaming with people. Other areas of medical investigation are fairly precise and far more predictable. But the human brain is such a complex organ that relatively little is known, when compared with what needs to be learned. We called in the best specialist available and he rendered his opinion that the damage was serious. "We'll just have to wait and see what happens," he said.

Each time there was a crisis, it had been possible to call in another specialist for his expert advice. But now we were at the point where there were no more specialists to call. Medical science had done what it could. The outcome now rested in the hands of a higher power.

We had known this all along. Nonetheless, I struggled with it. Many individuals patted me on the back and said, "Just remember that all things work together for good to them that love God." How often I had used that Scripture when speaking to others who were going through hard times! But how many of those times did I really comprehend the truth of what I was saying? Sometimes it seemed like an easy out when dealing with a person who was hurting and I didn't know what else to say. I felt sort of programmed to recite that particular passage. It certainly had been recited to me scores of times.

If it did nothing else, it caused me to think about it long enough to come to grips with its meaning. How can all things possibly work together for good? How can a marriage which has been destroyed work for any good? Or how can a human being who can no longer function in life, because of some tragic accident, work for good? How could some needless crime against an innocent victim work for good? Or how could the murder of a child work for any good?

Having memorized that verse from the *King James Version* of the Bible, I had always taken that translation quite literally. I had seen good come out of some circumstances, but I really didn't see how certain *things* could work for the good of anyone.

I was greatly helped when I began to look up Romans 8:28 in other translations. For example, the *New American Standard Bible* renders it, "And we know that God causes all things to work together for good." And the *New International Version* reads, "And we know that in all things God works for the good of those that love Him." This made sense to me. It's not the things that work for good. It's God who works in every situation. I could accept that in the dark situation we were facing. God was working for all of our good.

The weeks passed and Thanksgiving rolled around. It was an unusual time for us as we celebrated it with friends who lived only a block or so from the hospital. Every so often I trotted over to Tommy's room to see if anything new was taking place. I thought that Thanksgiving Day would be a perfect day for Tommy to wake up from the coma he was in. Each time I made that trip, it was with a sense of expectancy that this would be the moment Tommy would open his eyes, smile and say, "Hi, Dad." But it never happened.

Lois and I believed that at some moment, Tommy's brain would wake up and he would recognize us and all would be well. The deep purple was beginning to fade from around his eyes, and he began to move more on his own. Slowly he seemed to be coming around. Sometimes he even opened his eyes, but when he did he seemed to be asleep.

His friends made huge posters which we hung on the walls of his room. At times when his eyes were open, he would stare at them vacantly for long periods, but there was never any response.

At first, his wakeful times were few and far between. He opened his eyes for a short time and then tumbled back into his coma for several days before waking again.

One night, as Lois and I were with him in his hospital room, he suddenly cried out loudly. What excitement! "This is it!" we shouted. "He's come out of it." We ran to his side, both of us jabbering at once with tears running down our cheeks. But it wasn't. It was a cry of some kind, but we didn't know what it meant. Little did we realize, at that point, that the sound of crying would be the only response we would get for months to come.

"If we could just get him home," we thought, "with the family and the familiar surroundings, that would snap him out of it." As Christmas drew near, we became more and more excited about the possibility of having Tommy home for the holidays. Surely this would be just what he needed. If he could be home and hear our Christmas records and be with his brothers and sisters, that would pull him out of the pit he was in.

Christmas finally came, and in response to much pleading on our part, the doctor said that we could have Tommy home for the holidays. During the days just prior to Christmas, Lois and several friends spent hours every day trying to get a daily minimum of 1,000cc's of liquid food down his throat. He had been fed intravenously via a tube through his nose. But that caused infections so it became necessary to feed him by mouth.

It was a tedious and exhausting process. We had to feed him during one of those rare moments when he was awake and not crying. Since he had lost his swallow reflex, it took continuous effort to get enough food down him for him to survive. He was wasting away to nothing. Four out of every five spoonfuls of food would spill out of his mouth and run down his chin. Lois patiently spooned the food back into his mouth, trying to hold his mouth shut with one hand while stroking his throat with the other. This induced a swallow now and then.

Along with his food, he also had to be fed Maalox, a chalky liquid to prevent ulcers. He hated this. The one thing that seemed to go down the best was Imogene Booker's homemade ice cream.

We knew having Tommy home over Christmas would mean constant care and work for all of us, but we were confident that he would respond positively to familiar surroundings. Arrangements were made for him to be placed on a stretcher, loaded into an ambulance, and taken to our home. One of the Ecuadorian aides who took care of him came along as well. The house was adorned with every Christmas ornament we had. Tommy's favorite records were placed on the turntable. Our other children, who had not seen Tommy since the accident, were waiting to show their love to him.

He was carried into the house and placed on the couch. He rallied from his sleep, rolled his eyes vacantly around the room, cried, and sank back into unconsciousness. The children stared in confused disappointment. We stood stunned, sharing their dismay, but trying to prop up the mood of the moment with brighter prospects. Thus began the most difficult Christmas of our lives. The only time Tommy woke up was to cry. He was like a baby who couldn't express why he was crying, if there was a reason. We couldn't tell what he needed or where he hurt. We didn't know what to do. So we tried everything under the sun, but nothing seemed to work.

It was during this time that I began having some of my darkest days. Lois said that she didn't feel the weight of the burden so heavily because she was able to do something to help Tommy. But I felt too helpless to do anything. I felt too clumsy to try feeding him and useless to try anything else either.

Each day I ran to the Word for strength. But at night I was assaulted by the enemy. I could sense his presence in the room. Each time he came, he tormented me with the worst kinds of thoughts such as, "Tommy will never recover. For the rest of your life you will have to take care of him just like you are doing now. He is going to be a big man, and you will have to carry him and lift him for the rest of your life."

I had a bad back, and this thought was a nightmare. Suppose I became unable to do it? Who would take care of both of us when my back went? Dear Lois? That would be too much to ask.

I finally rose from my bed and rebuked Satan in Jesus' name. "Satan, you have no claim on my life, my thoughts, or my peace. I do not belong to you. I am no longer your slave, and in Jesus' name I command you to get out of my mind." Then I took my Bible and read and cast myself upon the Lord, putting myself in His hands. I read wherever my Bible opened. I said, "Lord, You know what my real needs are right now better than I do. Holy Spirit, guide me to the Word of grace I need to read right now." I was amazed at how the Lord answered those pleas each time. Time after time I went to Him like that, and time after time, He led me to just the right Scripture I needed.

I know full well that is not a good way to proceed in any kind of Scripture reading program. But given those circumstances, I didn't feel like saying, "I think I'll do a study in Ephesians," or "I think I'll do a topical study on redemption." I simply cried for help, and the Lord heard my plea.

I especially remember one time when the enemy began tormenting me with the idea that Tommy's recovery depended upon my faith. By that time we were physically and emotionally exhausted, and I felt that my own faith was stretched so thin it could help no one. The thought was frightening and horrible. Could there be any truth in that? I cried to the Holy Spirit for help and picked up my New Testament. I turned to Romans 3 and read. What first caught my eye was like a tonic of new life to me. "And what if some do not believe?" That was the question I was asking myself. I read hastily on. "Does that make the faithfulness of God of no effect? God forbid! Let God be true and every man a liar." Satan is a liar too. I cried tears of relief and joy. What a blessed reminder that God wasn't affected by my tired and discouraged faith. "Lord," I cried. "I may or may not have the faith to believe that You will heal my son, but I can believe in the certainty of Your faithfulness."

It was at that point I began to realize that from our perspective, we can only see things from the level of our circumstances. Our circumstances had been instantly changed and had become extremely difficult. But how good it was to know that He had not changed. He was still the same. He was in no way altered by our circumstances. He was the One who remained constant when all else was in a state of metamorphosis. Our trust is secure only when we place it in Him.

By Christmas I had fought and won that battle with Satan, but the realities of getting the food down Tommy's throat and taking care of his other needs were still as pressing as ever. In addition to the tedious hours of feeding him enough to meet his minimal needs, Lois and the aide spent endless energy changing Tommy's clothes and bedding because he was still incontinent. The casts and splints which still covered his body made this task difficult. And of course, he always cried.

Even his little brother Kevin, who was only four at the time, tried to help make Tommy happy. Of course, he didn't really understand what was going on, but he pulled up a stool next to the couch where Tommy lay, and leaning forward with his little face rather close to Tommy's he talked to him. When Tommy cried, he endeavored to cheer him up with positive reports of four-year-old news.

But such was our Christmas. The experiment failed miserably, and the disappointment of it almost wiped us out. We were exhausted. It had been so tiring for Tommy that when we took him back to the hospital, he slept for almost a week without waking up.

When he did awaken, however, he seemed to be a little bit more with it than before. But by now that had become a pattern. Each time after a rally, he would sink into what we called a "down time," and each time he woke up he seemed a little more present than before.

4
Return to Illinois

We approached the tenth week after the accident. Tommy had been in various phases of his coma for nearly six weeks of that time. The last four weeks had shown some real progress. He was eating much better and responding more. The medical staff was getting him up and sitting him in a chair for some time each day. He hated it and cried a good deal. My mom came to Ecuador to help care for Tommy and the other children. She was a terrific help and was great with him.

He was not speaking at all yet and had not even ventured as much as a smile. But he seemed to follow conversations with his eyes, and we thought that perhaps he was understanding what was being talked about. Mom was a good conversationalist and talked with him for long periods of time. She recounted her own personal experiences, talked about my childhood, reminded Tommy about things that he did when he was little, and generally did what she could in a totally one-sided conversation. As she spoke, Tommy would watch her and sip water through a straw.

One day she began telling Tommy about a recent experience she had been through while in Ecuador. We had taken her to Otavalo, a fascinating Indian market. It's a place where every Saturday the Otavalan Indians gather to sell their wares and buy what they need for their own use. These people are the weavers of Ecuador. They make tapestries and wall hangings, woven curtains and embroidered clothing, and sweaters and ponchos of various colors, sizes, and styles. The Otavalan Indian market is a must for any visitor to Ecuador, and we didn't want Mom to miss out on this opportunity.

Now, our kids have always been great tappers. Rather than call us by name, they would stand by our side and tap us on the arm until we acknowledged their presence. Then they would tell us what they wanted. Perhaps they acquired that practice because we had been careless about hearing them when they spoke to us. In any case, this habit had been one which bothered Lois to no end, and she was continually trying to break them of it. My mother had become accustomed to the tapping habit and was very patient about it.

While at the market, Mom was standing and looking at some sweaters when she felt a gentle tapping on her arm. She continued to look at the sweaters as she reached over and patted the tapper on the hand. Then she proceeded to put her arm around him, commenting on the merchandise as she turned to look at her grandson.

Suddenly she found herself face to face with the toothless, grotesque grin of an old Indian beggar man. Startled and horrified, she withdrew her arm with a squeal. The old man hobbled away laughing lustily.

Mom giggled like a schoolgirl as she relived the event for Tommy. He watched stonefaced for a moment, and then suddenly his face broke into a broad grin.

How good it was to see that smile again! We had wondered

if it had been lost forever. The currents of this new event quickly rippled through the hospital. It seemed that each bit of news traveled that way and was of utmost importance to everyone. Each victory for Tommy was a victory for us all.

Margaret and Travis Gowan came to HCJB at the same time we did. We had gone to a candidate orientation together, to language school in Costa Rica together, and had arrived on the field just four months apart. They had known Tommy since he was five and were among the first to be at our side when the accident occurred.

Margaret was one of the many who spent long and arduous hours trying to feed Tommy, during those first days after the tubes had been removed and he was learning how to swallow again. She was always a positive person noticing every little sign of improvement.

Right about that time, it occurred to Margaret that Tommy might be able to write out his thoughts to us. She found a pencil and pad and presented them to him. Almost immediately he began to write on the paper what looked almost like chicken scratches. Nothing more. Was this a reflection of what was left in Tommy's battered brain? At first it was a real letdown.

Margaret studied the hieroglyphics on the paper. In the center of all the scratching, she made out a word—MOM. It was no mistake. It was really there. How excited we were! It was like the excitement we experienced when, as a baby, he had said his first word, only much more so. For days he penciled his chicken scratches, and from time to time a word appeared.

One day among the scratchings a message appeared. "Phone to call Peter." Peter was a classmate of Tommy's from Norway, who did not know the Lord. Tommy had been very burdened for him prior to his accident and was determined to see Peter give his life to the Lord. We had all prayed for Peter as a family. Now, as much as Tommy's mind was able to function, Peter was still a primary concern for him.

We called for Peter to come to Tommy's room, and when he did I showed him the note. "Peter, I think there is something that Tommy would like to say if he could, but since he can't I will say it for him. Tommy prayed for you a lot before his accident, because he always regarded you as a neat guy and a good friend. He was concerned that you didn't know the Lord Jesus as your personal Saviour, and he wanted to share the Lord with you. He tried to do that himself, but didn't have the chance before the accident. I think he wrote that note because he still has that concern on his mind."

From there I proceeded to open my Bible and share the plan of salvation with him. He stared wide-eyed, somewhat taken aback by Tommy's silent presence in the bed and his inability to communicate. But he received what I had to say politely and thanked me for it. Then he left. Peter did not accept the Lord that day, and shortly thereafter his family returned to Norway. We still don't know about Peter. We can only trust that the burden which Tommy had for him was from the Lord, and that He will work out His plan for Peter's life.

At the end of 10 weeks, it had not yet been possible to set Tommy's bones. His brain injuries had been so severe that the most immediate concern was to get him stabilized. Surgery was, however, indispensible. Each time surgery had been contemplated, his temperature rose for some unknown reason and the surgery had to be cancelled. Each time the surgery was scratched, his temperature returned to normal minutes later. This occurred on several occasions, and the doctors were extremely puzzled about the reasons for it. We believe it happened because God had another plan!

Finally, the doctors urged us to take Tommy to the United States for further care. They had done all they felt they could in Quito, and said that if he were their son, they would look for help in the United States. Later we found out that the care he received in our missionary hospital in Quito had been excellent. They had done exactly what they should have. It was good to know that.

To move Tommy from Ecuador to the United States involved a very complex process. He would have to be flown on a stretcher, and the airlines have strenuous demands for stretcher patients. Doug Peters, our field director, shouldered the responsibility for finalizing these complicated arrangements which required numerous guarantees.

We had to have a release from the Quito hospital and a statement of acceptance from the hospital which would receive him in Wheaton, Illinois. The doctor who would treat him there also had to verify. Tommy was to be taken by ambulance to the Quito airport. Once he landed in Miami he would be received by trained ambulance personnel, and would remain in their custody during his time there. The ambulance attendants would then be responsible for placing him on the connecting flight to Chicago. There he would have to be met at O'Hare Field by a recognized ambulance service and be delivered by them to the hospital. All of these arrangements had to be guaranteed before the airlines would agree to transport him.

It was also necessary for us to purchase four first-class seats from Quito to Chicago, because the stretcher occupied two spaces and the airlines could not sell the adjoining seats. We could use those two seats for family members, however.

While all those arrangements were being made, we were trying to get the family ready to leave for an indefinite period of time. We hardly knew how to plan, although we were hoping that we would be back in six weeks or so. There were many things about Tommy's status which had not yet dawned upon us. The arrangements were finally in place, and 10 days after the decision was made to go stateside, we boarded the Braniff flight for Miami. It was January 13, 1976, a few days after Tommy's 13th birthday.

Ten hours later, Tommy was in his new home in Central DuPage Hospital. Dr. Paul Jorden, a veteran orthopedic surgeon in the Chicago area, agreed to accept Tommy's case. He made an evaluation of Tommy's condition, after looking at the many X rays from Quito and taking numerous new shots himself.

While Lois, Becky, and Tommy flew from Miami to Chicago, I remained in Miami with my mom and our other boys to pick up our Chevy van. We had left it in Miami to be shipped to the field, but because of importation problems, it had remained there for five months. Since we had to return to the States and needed transportation, I picked it up and drove the rest of the family to Chicago.

Most of the evaluation process had been completed by the time we arrived in Chicago, and Lois described all that had taken place. One of the more interesting things she told us had to do with the discovery Dr. Jorden made when he removed the cast from Tommy's left arm. As he cut the cast away, he saw a stump of bone protruding through the skin of his left bicep.

"What's this?" he queried. Further evaluation showed that the arm had been broken in two places between the elbow and shoulder. The short piece of bone between the two breaks, about three inches in length, had turned sideways and become fused to one of the bones in a horizontal position. Thus the end of it was sticking out through the skin. Since it was necessary to use a small portable X-ray machine in Quito, pictures were not taken of all the different angles. Thus this detail failed to show up.

It would be necessary to go into the arm, break or cut the

bone loose from where it had become fastened, freshen up the ends of the bone, and put them together with a stainless steel plate. There were several concerns. It was a dirty wound with the bone protruding from the skin, which meant that the opportunity for bacteria to enter the wound was ample. Very possibly, Tommy's body would reject the plate. His arm had been immobile for 10 weeks already and needed exercise and rehabilitation. Tommy wasn't able to move anything on the left side of his body, and he had little feeling in it. If the body rejected the plate, it would require 8 to 12 more weeks of immobility in order to heal, and he could lose the use of the arm by attrition. The picture was a serious one, but Dr. Jorden said that he would do his best. We all prayed fervently about the situation.

The plate was placed in his arm and we hoped for a positive result. However, we were not prepared for the result we got. In two weeks time the incision was healed and the scar hardly had a scab on it! Rehabilitation commenced almost immediately.

"This is amazing!" Dr. Jorden exclaimed. "Tommy's arm has not only accepted the plate, but it has healed from the surgery in record time. Truly, our prayers have been answered."

When Tommy came out from the anesthetic this time, he seemed more alert than before. He still couldn't speak, or move any part of his left side, but he began to respond to questions with more understanding. Given a choice of Coke or ginger ale, he could scribble his answer on a notepad. He could answer yes or no questions by raising one finger for yes and two fingers for no. For some of the medical staff he would signify yes by moving his finger up and down and no by moving it from side to side. And some required that he give those answers by shaking his head. He seemed able to sort out which persons required which kind of response. This was very encouraging to us.

He could recognize all of the family members without any problems at all, but he often did not remember others who had been close family friends for years. He never initiated any kind of communication, but he responded well to questions or information presented to him.

A speech therapist began working with him, and before very long he could whisper the answers to yes and no questions. Physical therapists worked with him daily moving his arms and legs, but there was still no sign of any control or movement on his left side.

There were two neurosurgeons who worked with Tommy. One of them was a Bolivian doctor by the name of Dr. Arana. He often spoke to Tommy in Spanish and was happy that Tommy was able to understand him. He stated that in cases of severe brain injury, the second language is often lost. The fact that Tommy seemed to understand Spanish was encouraging to him. He often came to Tommy's room with various objects of different sizes and colors and asked him for responses to his yes or no questions. Tommy liked him and worked hard to cooperate with him.

The other doctor was not encouraging at all. He was the one who was supposed to be the real specialist, but his view of Tommy's future was bleak, and he was of no personal encouragement to Lois or me. In fact, on one occasion, his prognosis was particularly grim. After about three months, Tommy's face began to droop badly on the left side. By this time we knew that he had lost the sight in his left eye. The optic nerve at the base of the skull had been damaged by the blow to his head. But when suddenly, after such a long time, the left side of his face began to sag, we were concerned. When he smiled, only the right side of his face smiled, and when he drank liquids, he began to slobber from the left side of his mouth. We sought out the doctor to ask his evaluation of this new symptom.

"Well, it looks like the brain cells are dying. It is the worst thing that can happen, but I am afraid it is irreversible." With that announcement, he strode off down the hall.

Lois looked at me, recovering from the blast of what we had just heard. "I don't believe it," she stated, refusing to be shaken. "I'm glad he doesn't have the last word. We'll just keep appealing to a higher power."

Later that afternoon the doctor recommended that Tommy be moved to nearby Marianjoy Rehabilitation Hospital. In his opinion, Tommy would remain paralyzed on the left side and would probably not regain much of his mental ability either.

Again we remembered the promise which the Lord had given. We preferred to claim God's promise for Tommy and look to the Lord for His help in the situation. We did not in any way depreciate the knowledge and skills of medical science, but we still believed that there was a God in heaven who understood His creation better than man could, and who had the power to intervene whenever it pleased Him to do so. Science had exhausted its store of resources, but we were still able to cling to the One to whom we had appealed so many times before.

As time passed, we were becoming more and more aware of the fact that our stay in the U.S. was indefinite. We could make no plans and no announcements as far as the future was concerned. It seemed that each new step of our lives was being prescribed by the medical profession. Yet, we were aware that we had come to the end of the line of the court of appeals to higher medical specialists because there were none.

Our family relationships all during this time remained strong. Each member of the family, from the youngest to the oldest, accepted without complaint the changes thrust upon us. The younger children understood our responsibility to be away with Tommy every night for a period of time and they never made that responsibility difficult for us. Becky was usually the one who ended up with the baby-sitting duties, but she never hesitated to do it and shouldered that job without any expression of discontent.

Lois and I maintained our relationship just as it had always been. Our marriage had been strong from the beginning and would continue to be so all through the ordeal. While there would be changes in our personalities and home responsibilities, the relationship that we shared would remain unaltered.

I have heard that in such difficult circumstances, some marriages tend to fall apart. I have asked myself why that would occur and have decided that those marriages were not strong in the beginning. The time to build a marriage is not when the stress is the greatest. That is the most difficult time to build it, although I know that it has been done. The best time to build a strong relationship is before all that added pressure is in evidence.

A strong marriage can take the heat of fiery trials better than a weak one can. The Lord provides grace to couples just as He does to individuals, if the two people involved are ready to receive it together. Lois and I have shared a mutual trust and respect for one another for many years. We have passed the stage where one blames the other for the problems that come into our lives. Neither of us ever sought to blame Tommy's accident on the other. Nothing could possibly be gained by that. I don't think that either of us felt that we needed more pity or sympathy than the other. I have always showed and expressed my feelings more than Lois does, but I know that I did not feel the hurt any more than she did.

And we shared openly with each other all during the experience. We did not hide our struggles or concerns, except perhaps at the very beginning when each was concerned not to add to the other's already heavy burden. We have never concealed our feelings from each other. We have never kept a record of grievances or offenses against each other. When there have been moments of tension or misunderstanding, we have dealt with them. We have always been quick to forgive one another and have never allowed ourselves to go to bed at night angry at each other.

If anything, there were fewer moments of tension between us, because we knew that we needed one another more than ever. I have been on athletic teams and worked in organizations where when things got tough, everyone started laying blame on the other members. That, of course, is the worst thing to do. When the chips are down and the way is difficult, it is time to close ranks and pull together. That is when we should recognize how much we really need each other. Lois and I really needed each other and we knew it. The family knew that we needed each other and that was the way it was.

The touch of Lois's hand was like strong medicine to my wounded spirit and I wanted to give her all the comfort and strength I could muster, although that didn't seem like very much at times. But I can never forget the moments that we lay in each other's arms at night and claimed the presence and promises of God together. There was never any dichotomy in our marriage. We carried our burden as one person.

5

A Slow Road Back

Many patients had been helped at Marianjoy. Some had re-gained much of what they had lost through strokes or acci-dents. But the staff had also dealt with those who never regained any of their physical or mental functions. Many of the latter were the victims of motorcycle accidents who, in a moment, were changed from normal human beings to quadriplegics who had no hope of returning to normal activities again. Tom was entering into a society where all of the residents were battling with their own limitations, learning what their new capacities were.

After our arrival at Marianjoy, the old master doctor quietly studied Tommy and his responses. He was a man who had worked with the most destitute of human misery. He was familiar with suffering and understood not only the suffering of the patient, but also that of the family. He spoke honestly, but measured his words carefully.

"Well," he said, "it is impossible to say for certain at this point, but I believe Tommy could regain some use of his left

side again. He may possibly be able to take care of himself—
that is, feed himself, wash his own face—things like that. We
will just have to wait and see what happens."

The hospital rules were very explicit. All patients had to be
dressed in street clothes during the day, whether they were
paralyzed or not. This was to help restore their sense of human
dignity which many of them had long since lost. This repre-
sented a tremendous amount of work for the staff since many,
like Tommy, had no control over themselves and had to be
changed several times a day. Patients had physical therapy
twice every day, once in the morning and once in the afternoon. In addition to that, some had speech and/or occupation-
al therapy; and those who needed psychological care also had
time built into their schedules for that. Patients were pushed
to the maximum and needed good periods of rest.

Partly for that reason, visits by family or other outsiders
were limited only to the evenings. Special visits could be planned
for some of the therapy sessions, but only on occasion. The
sessions were sometimes difficult to observe because of the
physical pain and mental anguish which resulted. While we
knew that Tommy would cry through each of them, we also
knew that therapy was necessary, and were glad that he was
in the care of professionals who cared about him. We were glad
too that we did not have to be there for all of his therapy
sessions. In fact, the entire schedule was good for us since we
now had more time with the other children, and could keep a
more regular schedule at home.

It became possible for us to take the rest of the family to the
center for evening game times. As Tommy began to speak
more, he was able to participate in several kinds of games
which involved the entire family. While his personality was still
very different than it had been before, the other kids seemed
to take it all in stride and were very good to him.

We began to understand that what we had thought he was comprehending was really over his head. His messages were often garbled, and his retention of new information lasted less than 10 seconds. In introducing him to a new person, I would say, "Tommy, I want you to meet my friend Gene. Gene, this is my son Tommy. Now, Tom, what is his name?" Tom would look at the person, and with his palms up he would shrug his shoulders indicating that he had already forgotten. We began to use that as a measure of Tom's progress.

We often talked about the many family things we had done with Tommy, such as going to Disney World. We expected him to remember an event like that. With a pleasant smile he'd listen to us tell about our Disney World escapades, but he remembered none of it. However, a few days or weeks later, if we began to discuss the same subject, he would suddenly remember quite a few things about it. This process would be repeated time and time again with varied topics of events and places that Tommy should remember. It was as if entire memory banks were waking as he recalled the memories and resources which were stored in them.

Each evening I asked Tommy, "Son, what did you have for supper tonight?" Often he shrugged his shoulders that he didn't remember. But later during a conversation he would suddenly render a verbal reply. "Chicken," he'd blurt out. The person who had helped feed him shook her head with a negative answer that he had not really had chicken at all. On one of those nights I asked him what he had eaten with the chicken, and he responded, after a puzzled look, "I think it's called the father of all green things." "Well," I said, "at least he hasn't lost his creative abilities."

Another night he wrote us a note which read, "I had dinner with Mrs. Pluck. She was very, very wet." Later we learned that he had eaten with a woman who was very fat, not wet.

Where he had gotten the name, Mrs. Pluck, we had no idea, but the substitution of one word for another became characteristic of his speech for quite some time.

Some of these comments were humorous, and of course, we all laughed together, but they were really quite frightening too. In the light of the neurosurgeon's prognosis, we struggled to dismiss some of the things which he had said, and allow the Lord to continue to work in Tommy's life. We were not really trying to put any words in the Lord's mouth, but we preferred to go by faith rather than by sight.

We wanted what God would do to be to His own glory, and we knew that each new step for Tommy was a victory and a sign of God's working in his life.

Chaplain Evan Welsh of Wheaton College was a good friend of ours, and had been for many years. The first time he ever saw Lois and me in each other's company was in the college bookstore. Lois and I had only known each other a few days, but when he saw us, his eyes lit up and he said, "Oh, I'm so glad to see you two together." From that day on he became our counselor and confidant. Our friendship grew strong— in fact, he performed our wedding ceremony following my graduation.

He knew how much our family loved little schnauzer pups, a love which we shared in common with the Welshes. One evening, as I arrived at Marianjoy, I saw Chaplain Welsh having a discussion with the hospital personnel. He was holding an adorable little schnauzer puppy and was pleading for permission to take it up to Tommy's room. That was definitely a departure from the normal procedure and against hospital rules. But after some discussion, a large towel was brought out and placed over the dog. I dashed up the back stairs so that I could be present when the entourage arrived. Moments later, Chaplain and Mrs. Welsh came through the door accompanied by a band of nurses, aides, and other personnel. They looked like important scientists with all of their assistants dressed in white following them into the room.

They had somewhat naughty but pleased looks on their faces as they knew they had pulled a coup of sorts. Once inside the room, they pulled off the towel and unveiled the furry little creature. Tom stared, wide-eyed, at the puppy. Then he smiled and reached out his hand to pat the wiggly little gray dog that smiled back at him.

"Tommy," we inquired, "do you know who this dog belongs to?" He looked at the puppy, then at the Welshes who stood by with happy smiles. With questioning eyes and a half-knowing smile at the corners of his mouth, he pointed to himself. Everyone laughed and cheered. It was one of those special moments when everyone knew that while protocol had been broken, the right thing had been done.

Each morning Tommy was taken to therapy. It was an ordeal for him every time, and he cried most of the way through it. But by the afternoon session, he forgot the morning's workout and was all smiles when his therapists picked him up for another round. While these work times were not pleasant for him, they were producing excellent results. He was beginning to move everything on his left side. At first he could barely move a finger or a toe, but once movement started, he progressed fairly rapidly.

Slowly his voice grew from a whisper into some audible tones. We were amazed to learn that during his silent months, his voice had changed from that of a boy to the lower tones of a teenager. Little by little, inch by inch, his body was waking up.

It was agony to watch Tommy go through all of this pain and suffering. Sometimes I felt furious inside. I never gave voice to those feelings, and I wasn't really angry with anyone in particular. It was just the whole situation we were in which caused those feelings to smoulder underneath. At other times I felt guilty about feeling angry. I spent extra time alone in prayer in order to deal with those emotions. I didn't want to let them grow into a root of bitterness. Actually, compared to many in that hospital, we had no reason for bitterness. We had, in fact, good cause for thanksgiving and praise for what the Lord was doing in Tommy.

One cold day in March, Lois and I drove to the hospital to observe Tommy's therapy session. This was our first visit to his therapy in many days. The agony of human suffering was everywhere. Individuals from all walks of life were there. A poor Hispanic family whose son was yet unable to speak or respond in very many ways was there. He was a young boy named Julio who had been a popular student at West Chicago Junior High School. He had been hit by a car in much the same way that Tommy had. Many of his injuries were identical to Tommy's, but after a full year he had shown little improvement.

I wanted to console his mother by letting her know that I understood the agony of her suffering, but when I endeavored to express that to her, she responded coldly, "No you don't. Your son is getting better." How difficult it must have been for her to watch Tommy's progress with the full knowledge that her Julio was going nowhere. She had seen many people come and go from this place, yet she and Julio remained, and time was running out. He would not be able to stay for much longer.

"There is no guarantee that Tommy will recover far," I thought. "Some Christians do suffer all their lives." I dismissed the thought and again referred to the promise in Psalm 91. I preferred to trust God in the darkness and give Him the chance to work, rather than to worry. Worry wouldn't help Tommy in the least. Only God could help him through all of this.

Another family came to the hospital regularly to see their husband and father. He had suffered a massive stroke and was unconscious. He was an attractive man with prematurely white hair. They had been such a handsome family whose lives had been completely altered by an instant. In all of the time that we saw them sitting by their father's bedside, we never saw any change in his condition. We wondered about this man and his beautiful family.

"How can people survive who don't know the Lord?" I often asked myself. The Lord was such a comfort and encourage· ment to us. What a blessing it was to experience the love of God and the comfort of Christian friends through this very dark time in our lives.

There was a woman there, a believer, who had been the center of family activity in her home. She was a super hostess, a great entertainer, and she loved to share her home and life with people all around her. Now, because of a stroke, she was handicapped and under orders to change her lifestyle. She was going home, not to wait on others as she had always done, but to be waited on. That would not be an easy change to accept, but she was a classy lady who knew Christ and recognized that she was not the victim of raw fate. The Lord still had a divine purpose for her life.

We also met a young man from Wheaton College who had broken his neck in a swimming accident and who was trying to regain some feeling and movement in any one of his four limbs. He was in one of the most difficult situations a young man can find himself, and yet we saw in him the presence of God. Seeing these people reminded us of the words of Corrie ten Boom, "There is no pit so deep, but that He is deeper still."

In that place, the rich, the poor, the young, and the old were all placed on an even footing in the struggle to regain some control over their own lives. There were no social barriers at

Marianjoy: all rejoiced in one another's triumphs, and all suffered with each other's defeats. The good news was exhilarating and the bad news was devastating.

But on this particular day, as we were taken to the center where Tommy was waiting for us, we had an extra amount of expectancy within us. He sat in his wheelchair, all smiles as we entered, ready to perform for us the tasks he had worked so hard to master during the past weeks. The therapist pushed Tommy's wheelchair to the end of the parallel bars and helped him to his feet.

The next 10 minutes contained all of the struggles of life itself. The therapist secured a heavy belt around Tommy's waist and placed herself firmly behind him for support. Then, clutching at the bars, wincing, crying, and almost falling, Tommy clawed his way along as his therapist urged, suppported, goaded, and prodded him to walk. Inch by inch, with faltering and spastic steps, trembling limbs, and fearful looks, Tommy moved from one end of the 15-foot bar to the other, crying all the way. His performance completed, his face broke into a tearful smile of accomplishment and pride.

It was wonderful but sad, ecstatic but agonizing, horrible but promising, all at the same moment. It was only one stride down the long road back to life, but it was a major step. He walked the length of those bars many times during the next weeks, and each time he did it better than the time before.

Soon after we arrived in Wheaton, I had said to a close friend, "Ed, we really need two miracles. We need a miracle for Tom to recover, and a miracle to pay off the bills. We were seeing a part of that first request take place as Tommy began to show steady improvement in his walking. We also began seeing progress in the area of finances.

Funds came in from many different sources. One friend gave us $1,000 in stocks. Another friend, from Jamaica, also sent

$1,000. There was a gift from the Samaritan's Purse, and HCJB set up a rehabilitation fund to which many of our friends and supporters contributed.

A part of that second miracle came through the person of Mark Clark, a young man from our home church. Mark was a lover of southern gospel music, and he was working hard to arrange a concert in the Wheaton area by the Kingsmen Quartet. Once the group agreed to come, the date and place were quickly set. The concert would not only satisfy Mark's desire to enjoy the music, but would also provide him with some financial rewards for his trouble.

From the time that he first heard about Tommy's accident, Mark started praying for him. One day as he was praying, the Lord began to speak to Mark about the inevitable financial needs that such an accident caused. The more he prayed, the more he felt that the Lord was leading him to do something to help meet that need. He decided to turn the gospel musical into a benefit concert for Tommy. We thought it was a beautiful thing for a young man to do. The promotion was done and the night of the concert arrived. The quartet was on schedule and Tommy was brought over from Marianjoy in his wheelchair. Many friends came to lend their encouragement and support to the evening.

However, Mark never arrived. He was riding his motorcycle to the concert when a car ran him off the road. He ended up in Central DuPage Hospital with a broken back. He lay in that hospital for over four weeks and had to wear a body cast for eight months. While the quartet did pay him a visit in the hospital, he never got to hear them sing in person. The best alternative available was to record the concert and play the tape for him. His project was a complete success as far as the concert was concerned, and as a result of it, a rehabilitation fund was set up for Tommy through MAP International in Wheaton.

What Mark did exemplified what the church of Jesus Christ does when needs arise within the fellowship of the saints. The HCJB Miami office also set up a fund for Tommy's rehabilitation; and with our medical insurance policies, the HCJB fund, and the fund set up through MAP International, the hospital and therapy costs were covered.

From the first news of the accident, many churches began calling Miami almost daily for news regarding Tommy's condition so they could pray intelligently for him. We received phone calls from the U.S. and Mexico, as well as cards and letters from people around the world who were praying for Tommy. How we sensed and appreciated that prayer support. One thing in particular that meant a great deal to me was the fervent, continuous prayers of children. Many of these little ones prayed for Tommy at every meal for a period of months and even years. Never again would I take lightly the prayers of children who pray with the kind of simplicity and faith that we are supposed to have. I knew that God would hear their prayers and I knew that He would respond to these whom He loved who came to Him in total trust, the kind of trust I often lacked. Through the years our faith accumulates excess baggage, but these little ones just take Him and His Word at face value.

During the first months after the accident, Tommy was not aware of much, especially not anything regarding the financial demands of the situation. But as he began to be able to think again, one of his first concerns was for the finances and how we were going to pay the bills. We have never discussed our finances much with our children, and we had been particularly careful not to mention this to Tommy. However, he suddenly became aware that the financial responsibilities were there. I don't know if he had any idea of how great they really were, but it was a major concern for him and he was continually apologizing for the accident. He mentioned it so frequently that we began to fear it might become a problem for him through life. The staff psychologist told us one of the common reactions of a critically injured person is guilt, and it seemed that this was true in Tommy's case.

Lois had kept a journal of Tommy's progress and of all of the friends and groups who had sent funds to help with the expenses of the accident. Finally, in order to ease Tommy's feeling of guilt and concern, Lois took the journal and read the list of names and gifts which had been received to help cover the costs. This seemed to satisfy his concern and he never expressed those feelings of anxiety or guilt again.

The journal served as a marvelous reminder for all of us that what seemed impossible to us, the Lord had under His management. How grateful we were for the Lord's faithfulness and for the love and concern of Christian friends who had allowed the Lord to work through them to meet our needs.

6
The Fellowship of Suffering

During this time in my Bible reading, I came to the Book of Job. I wasn't reading that book because of the situation we were in, but as I read about Job's trials I could in some small way empathize with him. I was comforted by God's faithfulness to Job, regardless of how grim the circumstances. At the same time I was comforted by the fact that our trials were so small by comparison.

I was reminded again of what our friend had said to me during those first hours after the accident: "The Lord must love you a great deal to trust you with something like this." That statement had been cooking on the back burner of my mind for months, but now as I read the account of Job's trials, it began to take on some substance. I read about that first encounter between Satan and the Lord. Satan, the accuser, complained that Job's faithfulness to God was due solely to the ease of Job's life. In essence, he accused Job of being a "rich Christian" whose faith had no substance and could not stand up to the rigors of difficulty or trial. But God knew Job and He loved him. God was willing to let Job demonstrate the real fiber of his faith and trust in God. Not only did God know that Job trusted Him, but God also trusted Job, and loved him to the point where He was willing to commit him and his faith to the perils of testing. A testing which would be surpassed only by what Christ Himself would endure as He carried out His redemptive work on Calvary.

I could hardly compare our trial with Job's, but for the first time in my life I could comprehend how the love of God and the suffering of His saints come together. I often spoke of trusting God as if it were some special virtue of ours. It is no great virtue for us to be able to trust in One who is so trustworthy. But for Him to trust us, when we fail so miserably and frequently, is indeed a wonder. The relationship which God has allowed us to have with Himself is amazing.

It is a partnership which exceeds our wildest comprehension when we consider that He trusts us to be co-workers with Him in the accomplishment of His divine purpose for the world. This is a part of the fellowship of His sufferings.

I was seeing a different side of trust which I had not recognized before, a side that perhaps through some trial of her own, our friend had been able to see prior to our testing. It did give an important perspective on our situation. Some people we talked to after the accident insisted that all suffering was against the will of God. They contended that no suffering occurred with His approval. They maintained that all suffering in this world was the work of the enemy and the result of man's disobedience to God beginning with Adam and Eve. It was part of the wasted fruit of sin. They told us, "Jesus suffered for us and 'by His stripes we are healed,' so that no saint ever need suffer again. If a child of God suffers it is because of sin, or unbelief, or because of some other spiritual weakness."

I know many dear saints who have suffered, and because of

their infirmities, their testimonies have been many times more effective than they might otherwise have been. I have no argument with the fact that God heals, and that this healing can take place because of Christ's redemptive work and His victory over sin and death through His stripes, His death, and His resurrection. But physical death is also a result of the Fall. "In Adam all die" without exception. The only ones who will be spared are those who will be translated when Jesus comes again. (See 1 Corinthians 15.)

The Apostle Paul suffered from some infirmity which he besought the Lord three times to remove. God in His sovereign wisdom decided to allow Paul to get along with the problem. Paul, on his part, accepted it as being part of the Lord's design for his life. Surely the Lord has His own reasons for what He permits in our lives, and we can be sure that it is in our best interest and according to both His love and His wisdom. (See 2 Corinthians 12:7–9.)

I have many friends who have experienced God's healing in their lives. Some have been healed in their bodies and some in their spirits which is equally miraculous, and I love when God heals people that way. During the years at HCJB we have seen some rather marvelous recoveries which we fully believe to be by the miraculous touch of God. But that healing has not come according to a prescribed formula. Rather it has been in accord with the divine providence of God for each person.

I believe the story of the Good Samaritan is in the Word to let Christians know that God wants us to demonstrate our concern for the suffering by doing what we can to alleviate pain and to care for the afflicted. It is an opportunity to demonstrate our love and express Christ's love to them.

That is why HCJB operates two hospitals in Ecuador and engages in medical caravans to remote areas where medical care is not readily available. Where we have the opportunity to minister to physical needs, we can minister to spiritual needs as well.

At the same time, we need to exercise caution that we don't add to someone's burden by making him feel that he is suffering because he is in some way deficient in his commitment to the Lord. Jesus came to take away our guilt. As Christians we should not want to make a fellow believer feel guilty because he is suffering. We want to uphold him and pray with him. Our great desire must be for the will of God to be worked out in his life, and we can trust God to make that will evident. There are many times when the will of God is different from our own.

We have a tendency in North America to think that God wants to bless us with perfect health, complete success, and financial prosperity. That idea is difficult for me to defend from the point of view of Scripture and very near impossible to sell in countries where there is a great deal of suffering and poverty. In most countries of the world, the majority of believers are in the lowest economic levels, and untold thousands are suffering because they are believers.

The mail we receive at HCJB from around the world describes a church which must measure its success by its faithfulness to Jesus Christ until the end, and not by the degree of wealth it possesses or by the absence of suffering. Only God knows how many have died for their faith in Southeast Asia and in Eastern Europe during this century. And if I understand my Bible, the number of martyrs will probably only increase. If we convince ourselves that being a Christian guarantees only the pleasant things in life, then when the hard times come, we wonder what happened.

I believe that God is my loving and most gracious heavenly Father. I believe that He cares about every detail of my life and wants to give me the best gifts. But the ultimate benefits of my redemption will be made manifest in eternity. And some of those will be determined by my faithfulness to Him in the face of adversity. And a part of His faithfulness to me is in the fact that I do not have to face those hard moments alone. He will never leave me nor forsake me; His grace is sufficient for my needs.

The Scripture teaches that "whatsoever is not of faith is sin" (Romans 14:23). I totally subscribe to this, and have to continually examine myself on that point. But faith does not lead us into ease. It leads us into eternal life, and it may lead us to suffer, if we are truly men and women of faith.

As far as our healing is concerned, the question is not always the presence or absence of faith. We love to be blessed with good health, but we may be blessed with poor health that we may understand the fellowship of His sufferings, endure hardness as a good soldier, and bring honor to God through the things which we suffer.

The basic question is whether we have the faith to believe that God's will is best and to trust Him to choose for us. Then, if the Lord leads us into trials, and He doesn't quickly deliver us from them, we don't have to doubt whether our faith is lacking.

We were not and are not ungrateful for the interest and concern of our friends who prayed for Tommy by the laying on of hands. One of the sweetest moments in the entire experience was when the elders from our little Spanish church in Quito came to the hospital and, anointing Tommy with oil, prayed for him. I believe that what the Lord is doing for Tommy today is in response to the prayers of people like that. I believe it was a biblical exercise that God is continuing to honor through His work in Tommy's life.

But while God does heal many by His own power and according to His sovereign purposes, some still suffer, and this suffering is never apart from His permissive will or His love. There can be great privilege and reward in suffering if we can learn to do it as Job did it, with absolute faith and complete dependence upon the will of God.

Tommy was making such a great recovery, in spite of the grim prognosis the doctors gave, that many of our friends were calling it a miracle. I didn't call it a miracle, although I didn't want to underestimate what God was doing in Tommy's body and brain. When the Lord performed a miracle in Scripture, He did the whole thing instantly and completely. What was happening in Tommy was happening because the Lord was doing an extra work of grace in him. I didn't for a minute want to take away from the good medical treatment and the loving, caring work of Tommy's therapists, but it was readily apparent that the Lord was restoring to Tommy many of the capabilities which had been lost. I was tremendously grateful for what God was doing and I wanted to give Him all of the glory, but I could not call it a miracle. Not while Tommy was still suffering, still struggling, and still far from being normal. For me to call it a miracle would be to make a mockery of the miraculous power of God.

Some well-meaning friends wondered if we were going through this ordeal because of some disobedience in the family. It was the sort of question raised in John 9:2 when Jesus' disciples asked, "Master, who did sin, this man, or his parents, that he was born blind?" to which the Lord answered, "Neither hath this man sinned, nor his parents; but that the works of God should be made manifest in him."

If anything were true, it was that our family experienced the greatest time of walking with the Lord that we had ever had. A few months before the accident we had turned our home into a hostel for vagrant young Americans, and hosted visitors from all over the world. Many came to know Christ, and some were set free from satanic bondage. The Spirit of God worked mightily in our midst and in our lives. With good reason, we had spirits of praise and often shared this joy with those around us to the point that some wondered if we had lost our spiritual equilibrium and had gone over the brink and into some kind of charismatic fanaticism.

It's amazing that if we say, "Praise the Lord!" several times in a row in more than a whisper, eyebrows go up in conservative Christian circles. I wonder how we'll say it when we get to glory where we'll repeat those praises for the ages of eternity. Perhaps God will ask us why we failed to praise Him more when we knew Him on the earth.

Nonetheless, several people had become concerned about us and about the way our spiritual development might be going, and in the end the matter had been brought to the attention of the board of trustees of the mission. We have always had a good board of directors and of course, they knew that the thing to do would be to go directly to the individuals involved, so we were invited to meet with our president, Dr. Abe VanDerPuy to answer the questions which had been raised.

Having worked in several different Christian organizations, I am tremendously grateful for HCJB and its policies. The mission has been true to the Word of God, has maintained a right sense of priority, has not been greatly affected by the trendy issues of the day in so far as its purpose is concerned, and is careful in matters of stewardship.

It has never compromised its biblical commitment to satisfy a donor or potential donor. On the other hand, it has not been separatist or sectarian, but has embraced the mainstream of evangelical Christianity. I do not know the personal backgrounds of many of my colleagues, yet I know where they stand in so far as the fundamentals of our faith are concerned.

The mission has been interested and concerned in the development of people. I believe it has endeavored to deal in love and has sought what is best for both individuals and families. So it was not unusual for Dr. Abe to meet with someone where a potential problem might exist. He always had a gift for "holding the truth in love" in matters where personal consultation was necessary.

Some months before Tommy's accident, I had been to dinner with one board member, a dear pastor friend who asked, "And if it is easy to praise the Lord now in the light of such blessing and sunlight, what will you do when everything seems to go wrong and the dark clouds of adversity envelop you?" To his question I responded, "I trust that I will be able to say, 'though He slay me, yet will I trust in Him' " (Job 13:15).

A few weeks later we were burglarized and many valuables were stolen. The most grievous loss to us were many photos of our children which could never be replaced. One of our checkbooks was stolen from the bottom of a box, and bad checks began to appear from all over Latin America. Three months after that, Tommy was hit. I found out what my response to trouble would be.

It was interesting that just prior to the accident, Lois and I had said, "You know, it's true. We have never really been through any great suffering." We had experienced great blessing from the Lord, and it hadn't cost us anything. We wondered how our faith would hold together in the darker moments of life. We would find out about that.

I had prayed, "Lord, whatever it takes to make me more like Yourself, do that in my life." I meant what I had said, but I did not know what it would entail. It was years before I dared pray that prayer again.

After the accident took place I sought God and said, "Lord, I promise to give You all the glory for what You accomplish through this, but I will not give You glory for what You do not do. This will be my opportunity to see You work in Your own way without my putting any words in Your mouth."

Perhaps that was an arrogant way to pray. On the one hand, I wanted what was reported when the whole thing was settled to be an honest history of how the Lord worked in our lives. I wanted what was done to be the will of God, and I wanted what was said about that to be a report on what actually happened. I didn't want to add anything to what He would do.

On the other hand, I now realize that I was being like Thomas who demanded to see the scars in Jesus' hand and to thrust his hand into His side before he would believe. I was trying to put God into some kind of test tube so that He could prove to me that He was in control and able to do the impossible.

However, when friends were telling Tommy to say that he was healed because of the laying on of hands, and others were calling his improvement a miracle, I was still waiting on the Lord for His final answer.

Tommy was having some struggles with his faith, wondering when it would be strong enough to see the visible results of the healing he sought and which was being promised. He wondered where he was failing the Lord. He continually sought God's forgiveness and that of others to insure that there was nothing in his life which would rob him of his healing.

At first we welcomed every individual who wanted to pray with him, but after a time, we began to protect him from those kinds of situations which we felt would only add to his struggles. Occasionally, however, some individual would slip into his room and seek to be God's instrument for his healing.

All these individuals meant well. We never doubted that. Neither we nor Tommy resented them. But with time, Tommy was coming to a new acceptance of himself and was content to wait upon the Lord for His will in his life. It was good to see him come to this place on his own, especially when we had watched him struggle through some tough battles. As time went by, Tommy began to accept himself and his handicaps better than others did.

7

Different
and Lonely

It was a chilly day in April when Tommy stepped through the door of Marianjoy Rehabilitation Center into the crisp air of the outside world. He had been in hospitals five months from the day of his accident, but now he was on his way home. Slowly, with the aid of a walker, he made his way to our car. He didn't have much grace or style in his walk, but he was walking, beaming from ear to ear as he went.

We still had a lot to learn about his condition. He was still quite helpless and needed assistance with absolutely everything. He was demanding too, and this was difficult for the other children to adjust to. They remembered him as he was before the accident and had only limited exposure to him afterward. He was more complex now, and they had to learn to relate to a different person. Tommy's friends went through the same adjustment. At first after Tommy came home, they would come to visit him, but it didn't take long before they stopped coming. Tommy became more and more lonely, and it was impossible to explain to him the reasons why.

Herein was the greatest struggle he faced and would face in the months and years ahead. He needed help with almost everything, had a terrible memory, and his existence was wrapped up in what he could see and touch. In some ways he was like a little old man whose world had shrunk to a microworld of aches and pains, dim horizons, and deep loneliness. Although he was demanding and impatient, he loved people, needed friendship, and felt tremendously rejected. Often he would say, "Why don't I have any friends?"

The whole situation was difficult for our daughter Becky, who made few allowances for Tommy. Our situation presented a whole new way of life for her and she wasn't sure how to handle it. During the first year at home she tended to remain on the fringes in school, not making many friends and hoping that soon we would be able to return to Ecuador. She resented Tommy's intrusions into her space. Tommy had no social life of his own, so he quickly inserted himself into everyone else's. This was sometimes awkward and embarrassing for Becky, as well as for the rest of the family, since he had forgotten many of the social graces, and we were never quite sure what to expect. The only thing that saved Tommy from total boredom was playing games, working puzzles, and watching television.

In spite of everything, we still did not comprehend how much damage he had suffered and kept thinking that once he got better control of his walking, and other body functions, he would be able to return to the ranks of the typical junior higher.

Becky decided to make the best of her situation and became totally involved at school. She was a super-busy teenager, an activist like me, with her own routine and schedule. Tommy's pleading for attention seemed to frustrate her. I often felt the same frustration. We both experienced a kind of anger which boiled up from time to time and manifested itself through impatient and unkind remarks. It wasn't really Tommy we were impatient with. It was the whole situation, but inevitably Tommy bore the brunt of it, and we often felt guilty about it. It was unsettling and upsetting to watch Tommy go through his bouts with loneliness, as well as his other suffering. Sometimes I was sure we were more a part of the problem than the solution. Tommy often asked, "Why doesn't Becky love me?" or, "I wish I had a better relationship with Dad."

In reality we all ached with love for him and wanted to help him. Unfortunately, our desperate love took the form of suggesting, correcting, and demanding that which we thought would make him more normal. None of us were able to grasp the fact that a helping kind of love wasn't a matter of planning, programming, or developing his return to some kind of normal behavior. It wasn't even a matter of his being normal at all. It was a matter of accepting him as he was and giving him the time he needed to recover from what he had been through.

Until Tommy came home from the hospital, the Lord had protected Lois from thoughts about what his future might be like. Now having Tommy home with constant demands for help and seeing his ineptitudes and inabilities, the most difficult period began for her. She was with him almost constantly. He asked the same questions over and over again, and developed certain mannerisms which were maddening. His whole world focused solely on himself to the point where he could not relate to anything which was not his or did not involve him personally in some way.

Lois found herself continually submerged in Tommy's subculture, and it was frightening and difficult for her. Tommy had always been a mama's boy, and now he expressed to her alone many of his feelings. She had the job of trying to relate these to the rest of the family.

Tommy's times of real discouragement and depression usually were at night. He would come into our bedroom with an exceedingly downcast look and want to talk about his loneliness, his longing for a friend, or his struggles with why the Lord was allowing all this to continue when he was praying so faithfully and diligently about it. The fact that others, even his family, had trouble accepting him as he was, made it more difficult for him. He even had grave doubts about whether God could accept him.

At times like that I found myself saying, "Lord, why did You leave Tommy here anyway? Certainly for him it would have been better had You taken him home to be with Yourself. He would experience no pain, no sorrow, and he would feel totally accepted in Your arms."

Then I would remember Psalm 91: "For the Lord says, 'Because he loves Me, I will rescue him; I will make him great because he trusts in My name. When he calls on Me, I will answer; I will be with him in trouble, and rescue him and honor him. I will satisfy him with a full life and give him My salvation' " (LB). We had claimed that verse as a promise from God, and had determined that we would continue to look to Him in spite of the circumstances of the moment.

In May, Tommy enrolled in the Wheaton Christian Grammar School with the same class he had been a part of during our furlough a short time before. Many of the students and teachers had faithfully prayed for Tommy and had supported him by visiting him in the hospital during those early weeks in Wheaton. The kids dutifully tried to be sympathetic with Tommy, and the teachers were very understanding. His memory was so short, however, that he would ask questions within minutes of having asked them before. His mind was filled with questions all of the time, but he seemed incapable of figuring out any of the answers. His hand stood in the air like a flagpole all through class. This behavior only alienated him from his peers.

At home he was one question after another. He couldn't do

any thinking for himself, and totally depended on the thinking of other people. His world turned in on itself, and he became trapped inside, aware of only those things which were going on in his immediate sphere.

But he did love to please us. He worked very hard in therapy and the greatest reward for his accomplishments seemed to be our approval of what he had done. Therefore, if we showed any disapproval of his actions or behavior, it was devastating to him. But it was hard to show approval when he sat for hours picking the lint from his sweater or trousers, or picked at the armrest on the couch until it had a hole in it.

The result was that he basically got two kinds of conversation hurled at him. That which praised him to the sky for the great progress he was making in some area, or that which instructed him how to be more like everyone else. There was little to talk about in-between. Our lives were arranged and ordered by the kinds of things that he could or could not do. And he was the center of most conversations.

He listened in on other people's conversations and offered unsolicited and often unwelcome comments. Irritated, we'd snap, "Tom, don't get involved in other people's conversations." Looking a little hurt, he would reply, "But I don't have any conversations of my own."

Shortly after he had returned to school, it became apparent that his schoolwork was almost too much for him. After some extensive testing and evaluation, we learned that his mathematical knowledge had been completely erased to the third-grade level. We also learned that other subjects had been wiped away, so we made arrangements for him to be tutored in math, English, and social studies by a certified tutor who lived just two doors away.

Tommy walked to her house. While it took me about 30 seconds to walk from our house to hers, it took Tommy a full

45 minutes to make the trip. He walked down our sidewalk to the street, turned left and passed the two houses to her sidewalk. Then he slowly made his way to her door. It would have taken much less time to walk across the lawn but, even though the terrain was fairly flat and smooth, the slight ups and downs and the soft grass made walking impossible for him. He even had trouble walking on shag carpeting indoors.

Several of the neighbors stated that they got their daily inspiration watching Tommy make that tedious journey from house to house. In spite of the time it took, and the effort it must have been, we cannot ever remember hearing him complain about having to do it. His daily motivation was in cutting a second or two off the time it took him to do something.

In the morning he made the tedious trip from the car to the classroom, and every afternoon, the arduous journey from our house to the tutor's. His physical therapy consisted mainly in walking and basic maneuvering and took all the strength he could muster. By bedtime he was exhausted to the point that he could never wake up to use the bathroom, and so most days Lois would have to change his bed. But little by little and with time, we began to see improvement in that area too.

8

A Family
Vacation

As soon as school was out we received an invitation to spend
some time with friends at their cottage in Canada. The LeMaires
had been special friends through the years. We taught together
at Wheaton Academy before going to Ecuador. Gene was the
one who had made most of the arrangements for our family
and for Tommy's placement in the hospital upon our return.
They had visited us in Quito the year before Tommy's accident, and we had enjoyed their visit so much. We went places
together and enjoyed Ecuador's rich, beautiful countryside.
Gene LeMaire was the closest to a brother I ever had.

Tommy's doctor felt that this vacation would be good for all
of us, after the difficult months we had just gone through. We
were still coming to grips with Tommy's real situation. Now
that he was at home, we were learning more and more about
the results of his injuries. In the early wakeful stages, Tommy's
world was entirely internal. Very slowly he began to extend
himself, but only as far as his arms could reach. Gradually his
world began to grow to include the room he was in.

When we began the trip to Canada, his world had extended to only what was within the car. There was a beautiful world to see outside the car, but it was beyond his scope of vision. He was still adjusting to having vision in one eye rather than two. But the whole matter was frustrating to us. How could he not see something as big as a mountain or as beautiful as a lake? But he simply could not see them, nor were they of interest. We hoped the time at the cottage would awaken him to the world in which he lived.

The LeMaires' cottage lay across the lake from the landing. The road ended at the landing parking lot, and from there many of the residents of the lake, after making a few final purchases from the little store, moved out across the lake by boat to reach their cottages and homes. Aylan Lake is one of the most beautiful lakes that I have ever seen and has 75 miles of shoreline. Most of the residents only spend their summers there since the winters are severe. The lake is near the little Polish settlement of Barry's Bay which is approximately a two-hour drive north of Peterborough, Ontario.

Tommy could not yet walk over anything other than flat ground and had to be carried almost everywhere. While we wanted him to walk as much as possible, I often carried him just to save time. Tommy was beginning to put on weight, and it was good to see his emaciated form regain some of its former huskiness. But he was heavy to lift and my back ached continually from carrying him. Because we were by the lake, I had to step in and out of the boat with him. Finally, I learned how to drop his feet over into the boat and then set him on the seat to put him in. To pull him out, I first got out myself and then pulled him out by grabbing him under the arms and raising him out until his feet finally came up onto the pier.

Regardless of the difficulties involved, we were happy to be together as a family in these beautiful surroundings and with our close friends. We could relax and take time to do whatever we wanted. We could sit by the lake or by the fire, or we could take walks with Tommy in the woods as long as two of us walked one on each side of him and supported him. The forest paths were uneven and covered with roots and stones, and proved to be a constant hazard for Tommy.

We arrived in Canada on Thursday. On Sundays many of the residents held church services up on a hill which overlooked the picturesque region. "Surely Tom can't manage to navigate that hill," we said. So we decided not to take him to the church service. He wasn't happy about that decision, and it became a challenge to him. He wanted to go to that church and he wanted to climb that hill. It seemed too ambitious to me, but he insisted. On the one hand, I had enormous doubts about whether he could make it, but on the other hand, I was thrilled to see his world expand and to see him so animated about attempting a rigorous hike.

After a few days of his insisting, we loaded him into the boat and sped across the lake to the boat dock at the foot of the chapel's hill. Getting out of the boat, we found ourselves standing at the beginning of the path which wound up the hill to the little open-sided chapel which overlooked the lake. Slowly we snaked along the winding trail which wended upward along the gentle slopes of the hill. Tommy was doing just great. Up and up we hiked until we rounded the last bend and climbed to the flat summit where the chapel stood.

What an exciting moment! The satisfied smile on Tommy's face was something to behold, as was the lake which stretched itself below us like a giant shimmering carpet. The sun's rays in the trees and the shadows on the ground around all seemed to add their approval to this special occasion. We sat down and prayed and thanked the Lord for what He was doing, and for this milestone in Tommy's progress.

Going down, we learned, would be much more difficult for Tommy. But as he walked he began to gain confidence and preferred to walk more on his own. I was right beside him so that he could take hold of me whenever he needed help over the rough spots. Progress was exceedingly slow, but we had all day and there was no rush.

Suddenly, his foot slipped on a small round pebble which rolled out from under him, and before we knew what had happened, he was sitting on the ground crying. He had gone down so easily that I was not too concerned by his crying. That had been characteristic of him since he had been in the hospital and usually didn't mean that any great damage had been done. "My leg! My leg!" he wailed. "I think it's broken."

"Inconceivable," I said to myself. "He couldn't have broken anything just by sitting down on the path. He really didn't fall that hard."

"My leg! I broke it, Dad. It's broken. . . . I can feel it."

"No, Tom. I'm sure it's not broken. You didn't fall that hard. Let's get you up so you can stand on it. That will help."

But as I took hold of his leg to straighten it, since he had sat on it when he went down, I felt the ends of broken bones rubbing together. A cold chill went over me. "I don't believe it, Gene! He wasn't kidding and he wasn't wrong. It is broken."

I wanted to join Tommy and cry with him. How could this be happening? How much more could one young boy take? He was just beginning to walk again, and it had been such a glorious morning. This would set him back for months. "Oh, God, let me wake up and find out that this is just a bad dream. Please, let me find out that it just isn't so."

I sat down beside Tommy on the path and tried to make him as comfortable as possible and to encourage him, though I was near depression myself. Gene ran off down the hill and took the boat to the landing to get a stretcher. We loaded Tommy in the boat, crossed the lake to the landing, and placed him in Gene's station wagon to take him to the hospital in Barry's Bay. There, the local resident doctor took the necessary X rays and set the fracture. Hours later we returned to the lake, Tommy's leg wrapped in a heavy plaster cast. It had been broken completely in two, in the left femur. He would have to walk on crutches, and this would prove to be very difficult, due to his previous fractures and the fact that his coordination was still so poor. It would take him some time to get the process together in his mind.

Through all the trauma he had endured thus far, Tommy never showed any sign of real doubt concerning his accident. He had completely accepted the fact that God was in control and that He would work out His plan for his life. At times, this acceptance concerned us. He had been through so much without a trace of inner struggle. But with this new development, Tommy's inner anguish began to show. "I can accept the fact that God can use my accident for some good purpose, but how can this possibly add anything to it? Why did He let me break my leg on top of everything else?"

That was a good question, and I didn't have any answers for him. He verbalized perfectly what I had been afraid to express. An internal battle was raging inside me, and I was not in a position to be of any help to him at that point. I admitted to him that I really didn't have an answer to his question. But I impressed upon him the fact that it would be necessary for both of us to believe through blind faith that God knew what He was doing, both in that which He ordained and in that which He allowed. From our perspective, we could neither see nor understand the plan and purpose of God through this newest setback.

Tommy had been immobile for such a long time that what he really needed was activity, not another long period of immobilization. The remaining three weeks at the lake were a mixed blessing. We were together as a family in the most beautiful surroundings imaginable. But activities were greatly restricted by Tommy's broken leg. We had taken a friend of Tommy's along to keep him company, but he really enjoyed the other young people more. Consequently, most of the time Tommy was alone while the others at the lake water-skied and enjoyed the many other things available for them to do. While they ran here and there, Tommy sat in the cottage and worked puzzles, picked lint off his clothes, slept, and experienced boredom, while he waited for someone to come and be with him. We played games with him and tried to include him in our conversations, but he really wanted the company of people his own age. The evenings were more pleasant for him because the outside activities were not available, and he was included in the games which everyone played.

It was a time that we all needed, a real therapy for the family soul. We carried him up and down the mountain each Sunday morning so he could continue to enjoy the chapel services. The LeMaires did everything that anyone could possibly do to make it a real vacation. We still look back to that time in Canada as a turning point for us.

On returning to Wheaton, we discovered that it was possible to trade Tommy's plaster cast for a lightweight plastic one which would allow him to swim. It was relatively small in size, weighing about one-fourth the weight of the plaster cast. In the water, its density was very similar to that of human matter. He was able to swim quite nicely with it and did so every day. After each swim he would take a hair dryer or a vacuum cleaner and blow the air through the porous cast until it dried.

A family friend and former HCJB missionary kid, Nathan Steele, took him swimming each day. The therapy did wonders for Tommy's endurance and progress. The swimming strengthened his body functions and he got to the place where he could swim 40 laps in a single night.

Tommy respected Nathan, and Nathan was great for Tommy. He pushed Tommy just a little more every day. Tommy would come back from each session with some new accomplishment, and that was good for his mental outlook and self-esteem. It must have been a shock for the other swimmers at the pool to see Tommy arrive on crutches, his leg in a cast, and promptly jump into the water.

During the next school year, Tommy made significant improvement. Tom Harvie, his eighth-grade teacher, required the students to memorize a new Bible verse each day. This was a real task for Tommy, but good exercise for him. Memory remained a problem for him for years, but the discipline of working on those verses was a big help in getting things clicking again. He worked hard on the verses at home, then looked at them just before saying them. But he got through them and profited from it all.

While Tommy slowly improved, we experienced the discipline of waiting. We had stopped expecting any sudden recovery, but settled for one little improvement each week. As long as there was some improvement to notice, we were encouraged. And there was always a new sign, although some of those improvements would almost drive us nuts. For example, fairly early in his therapy he kept trying to snap his fingers. We were all excited when he was first able to snap the fingers of his right hand. We were doubly happy when he was able to snap the fingers of his left hand. What we didn't know was that he would snap his fingers for years after that. And the snap, snap of progress became one of those things that we continually asked him to refrain from doing.

9
A Time
of Change

Prior to Tommy's accident, I was the Director of Broadcasting at HCJB and had numerous ideas which were in various stages of development. I was known as an idea person with all of the strengths and weaknesses that it implied. Most of the ideas meant a fair amount of work, but I tried to make them success-ful. One of them was related to a study program with the Wheaton College Graduate School. We arranged for a master's degree program in Communications to be taught at HCJB, and about 20 individuals became involved.

Numerous other projects related to broadcasting were in the hopper, and still others in the dreaming stages. I was happy with all of the activity which these things brought about, and never had time to be bored.

After Tommy was hit, all of these things went up in the air, as far as I was concerned. Instead of being of utmost impor-tance to me, they hardly mattered at all. It's amazing how our sense of priorities can be completely rearranged in moments.

Now, instead of being busy with activities, I found myself in

Wheaton waiting for Tommy to get better. I was also waiting for my own life's direction to come back from wherever it had gone. At one moment I desperately wanted to return to Quito; but at another, I didn't know if I wanted to return at all. The question loomed larger each day as to whether it would ever be possible to return to the mission field. I had felt called to missions and that was where I wanted to be. Now we were on the shelf waiting to see what the future would bring, and we didn't know how to get off.

My missionary call had been a traumatic experience. During my freshman year at Wheaton College, I had gone to see a missionary film which told the story of five young missionaries who gave their lives in Ecuador to reach the Auca Indians. I well remember watching the film with the critical mind of a college freshman, wondering why Christian organizations didn't produce films that were more professional. That was a pet peeve of mine at the time. I sat analyzing what, in my critical opinion, was a poor production, not realizing what was happening to me. Suddenly, I became acutely aware of a world in terrible need of the Gospel. I saw the lostness of man and the fact that I possessed useful knowledge that could help. I was ashamed. I wanted to run somewhere. Tears poured down my cheeks. When I left the meeting I went to my dorm, shaken to the roots of my being. "I will pack my footlockers," I thought. "I will catch a freighter and get to South America as soon as possible. Why should I waste my time studying?" I reasoned. "There are people who are lost out there and have no knowledge of the love of God. And now there are five fewer workers."

My friends hardly knew what to do with me. They called Chaplain Evan Welsh who said, "Tom, if you arrived on the mission field in your present state of mind, I'm afraid it would take the other missionaries away from their important work to try and help you. Why don't you just wait until the emotional effect of this has worn off. Then, when you are able to think with a cooler head, if the great desire of your heart is still to go to the mission field, I think you can know that you have been called of God."

That was such wise counsel. I did wait, and when the emotions had settled, I still had the desire in my heart to go to the mission field. I changed my major from music to anthropology, and from that day forward pursued my goal. Lois shared the same sense of God's calling.

Now we were sitting at home in the U.S.A. wondering if our missionary career had ended. We always said that we would remain on the field until we felt the Lord calling us back, in the same manner that we had sensed His urging us to go. Could this be His call to return to the States? I doubted that it was.

Perhaps as a result of our situation, I entered early into what has come to be known as a mid-life crisis. Whatever it was, I entered into a time of my life such as I had never experienced before. I am sure that there were scores of good opportunities for meaningful involvement all around me, but I couldn't seem to see them. I had no great desire to plunge back into the stream of activity, even though I was typically known to sink myself into work of some kind or other. It probably would have been better had I given myself to some sort of ministry, but I did not.

I became quiet and introspective. For those who knew me well, this was a difficult change to cope with. My friends, family, and associates were all patient and sought to involve me in meaningful ways. Perhaps the quietness of those days was not altogether bad. For the first time in my life, I dedicated a majority of time to deep and often meaningful contemplation. And I am sure that the changes which finally resulted in my personality and nature were not bad. Some people told me that they saw positive traits in me that they had never seen before.

Perhaps this was my time to be on the back side of the desert for a time, as Moses and Paul had been.

Nonetheless, I felt like I was in a state of suspended animation. I didn't really know where I was coming from or where I was going. There were some alternatives for me to choose from, but none of them interested me. I was having an identity crisis. I wasn't depressed over it, just waiting. Waiting and wondering if I would get excited about anything again. I was being taught the discipline of patience—a lesson I no doubt needed to learn.

All of this waiting made some interesting changes in our lives. My activities slowed to a near stop and I was not attracted to anything in particular, insofar as new involvements were concerned. As I became more quiet, Lois became more outgoing. Whenever we went out with friends, she carried the conversation. That was a switch. I had always been the conversationalist, and she the more reserved one. Now we had reversed roles, so that she was more the leader and I more the follower. That was no problem for me. In our relationship, what one lacked, the other supplied. While we never discussed or planned it that way, or got very philosophical about our relationship, in reality it always worked that way. It was one of the more beautiful parts of our marriage.

Lois had also begun taking some art courses at a junior college and was loving it. She was doing very well and growing all the while. My satisfaction came not from my own projects, but from watching her progress. One of the great joys of my marriage has always been in watching Lois grow. When I first met her she was a quiet person. Not shy, just quiet. She had been on her own, living off and on in a home for missionary children since she was eight. Her parents were missionaries in China until it closed. Then they were transferred to the Philippines. To a degree, Lois lost herself in a world of books. She worked to help meet her own needs, and generally learned to look out for herself. But she was quiet.

When I first met her at Wheaton College, she had a pronounced stutter which was the bane of her existence. Perhaps because of her stutter, she became a great listener. She tended to keep quiet in group situations unless she was with close friends.

When I met her, it was almost love at first sight. By the end of our first date, I returned to my room and informed my roommates that I had found the one I had been looking for. If I was sure about that, she was equally doubtful in the beginning, but with time our relationship grew.

We worked as youth directors in a little church in Naperville, a town a few miles south of Wheaton. As youth director, Lois had to give the missionary stories each Sunday morning. That task caused her no end of grief because of her stuttering problem. It was, however, great therapy for her.

As a missionary child who had been out of the home much of her life, she wanted to teach missionary children. She believed that the Lord has called her to do that, but she couldn't talk without that stutter.

Her mother wrote letters of encouragement to her and reminded her, "In quietness and confidence shall be your strength" (Isaiah 30:15). She knew her mother's prayers were close to her, and she never doubted that unseen support.

But each Sunday morning she struggled through the missionary story, and each Sunday as we drove back to the college, she tearfully asserted that she could not do it again.

"Oh, yes," I would say to her. "Next Sunday you must do it again." Through prayer and work, and with increasing confidence, her stuttering disappeared.

Now, I looked at her with admiration. She was carrying most of the conversations with our friends. No one knew the story of her struggle because no trace of the former problem remained.

While I still waited for some sort of direction for my life, opportunity presented itself for Lois to teach art in the Wheaton Christian Grammar School. She enthusiastically accepted. It was therapy for her and a needed relief from the pressures of our circumstances. She was being stretched in the positive sense. She loved the art classes, the children and teaching. The students loved her, and each day after school there were kids in the art room working on various projects. The halls were constantly filled with the colorful displays of the students' handiwork. When outsiders entered the school, it made them feel that something very good was going on there.

In the earlier years of marriage, we had been known as Tom and Mrs. Fulghum. Now, as a result of using the many skills which were exclusively hers and in which she excelled, she had an identity all her own. In that school we were known as Lois and Mr. Fulghum.

Meanwhile, we wondered if Tom would always be with us or if he would be able to carry on some life of his own. We prayed a lot about Tom's future and we prayed about our future as a family. By this time we knew that Tom would have some permanent handicaps, but we didn't know how many or how severe they would be. He was blind in his left eye, one leg was an inch shorter than the other, and he had motor problems on the left side of his body. In many of these areas, physical and mental improvement could take place for up to 10 years, especially if he worked at it. But I couldn't sit around and wait for 10 years to see what Tom's future would hold. I had to get back to work. I needed the kind of a job where I could get up early in the morning, get ready and go someplace—to an office, or a shop, to some kind of fruitful activity.

Eventually a position opened up at Wheaton Christian High

School where I had taught before going to Ecuador. It was good to be in touch with the young people again, and Becky and Tom were in my music classes.

During the next two years, Tom made steady but slow improvement. We were convinced this was the environment he needed for that time in his life, but during the two-year period I began to grow more restless. I enjoyed my teaching, and I managed to complete the requirements for my masters degree in Communications, which I had begun prior to Tom's accident, but I was feeling the need to move into some missions-related function. I was particularly interested in mass media. Knowing we couldn't return to Quito, we asked God for clear guidance.

Several opportunities opened up for us. One involved managing a large denominational communication outreach. Also, I had the option of teaching communications on the college level and had received inquiries from five different colleges. There were possibilities for ministry at a couple of churches, but none of these held for me that certain ring of the call of God.

One spring morning, I received a phone call from evangelist Luis Palau, who needed someone to help with a crusade effort in Scotland. This was the pull I had been praying for. After HCJB agreed to lend us to the Palau Team, we were off to Oregon where we spent a year in the beauties of the Northwest.

However, the decision to move to Oregon also had its difficulties. Becky had reached her senior year in school. The sudden move from Quito had been rough on her. When we first came home, we thought that Tom would be ready to return to Ecuador in six months or so. Becky, expecting to be a short-term student, had not jumped into the school's activities with great enthusiasm at first. But by now she was totally a part of all that went on there. She had many close friends, was a cheerleader for the soccer and wrestling teams, and was involved in just about everything. A move to Oregon at this time was not a happy option for her. Nor was it a pleasant thought for the rest of us to leave her behind, but it was a decision which had to be made.

Becky always carried the strongest personality in the circle of our children, and when she was at home, she was usually the dominant influence among the children. All our other children are more quiet and sensitive. As we thought about the total situation, we decided it would be best for her to stay for her senior year and graduate with her friends. And Tom might have a better chance to come out of himself, as the senior member of the children at home. After much prayer and some struggle, the decision was made for Becky to remain with friends in Wheaton, if she chose to do so.

Inevitably, our children must leave the nest, but we were not prepared for that to happen so soon. Our family has always been a close one, and this first departure from the group was hard for all of us. Karen and Kevin were especially torn by the experience. I remember saying good-bye to Becky as bravely as I could. Then, while she said her good-byes to the rest of the family, I walked around to the other side of the car and wept.

Becky did exceedingly well during her senior year, and Tom began to develop some leadership with the other children. The decision, though difficult, was a right one, and everybody grew as a result.

If the move resulted in a change for Becky, it resulted in an equally big one for Tom. For the first time in his life, he would enter a public school. Furthermore, he would be in a school where he knew absolutely no one and where no one knew him or the circumstances which had made him the way he was.

The Aloha Oregon public school system had a tremendous special education department, and Tom was received with open arms. The staff committed themselves to work with him in all the areas of his development where he needed help. At the outset, rather extensive testing was done to see what his potential was at that time. While the testing still showed large needs in the areas of math and science, Tom maintained a great capacity in the language arts. He had developed a stutter and was therefore placed in drama, a good relational and practical course for his needs.

During that first year, Tom had many difficulties in relating to his peers. He continued to be demanding and to ask too many questions. He was a loner in school, although he desired friends almost more than anything else. By the end of the year, the students in his drama class awarded him the "Burn Award." This was in no way complimentary, although Tom received it graciously.

Meanwhile, Tom applied to work at Camp Sambica in Bellvue, Washington for the summer. This was a major step for him to be out of the home for 10 weeks and with young people his own age in a camp situation. The camp administration was acquainted with Tom's story and was willing to give it a try. We were both excited and afraid of what the summer might mean to him. It could be a tremendous growing time. But he needed success, not failure, in this endeavor.

During the time that Tom was in camp, Lois and I were in Scotland for the Palau Crusade. We were gone for one month and often prayed for Tom in his new venture. When we returned, we were delighted to find him having a great summer, and the camp management satisfied with the contribution and the progress he was making. We rather expected that he would be calling home every few days; but he rarely called, except on those occasions when he knew that somebody would be coming his way and could bring him something he needed.

All during this time Tom often responded to altar calls for

commitment or for service. He continued with such a beautiful spirit toward the Lord and never seemed to experience any root of bitterness toward the person who hit him and left him in the road to die that night.

With summer over, Tom returned to school in Oregon. His camp experience had produced a new spark in him. He enrolled in drama again, and by the end of the first grading period, his teacher remarked, "The difference between Tom last year and this year is incredible! It's like two different people. He is less critical and demanding of others, he is easier to teach, and is more self-motivated. He gets along much better with his peers and asks fewer questions."

For the first time since we had left Quito almost four years earlier, we began to wonder whether it might be possible to return. But what if we were no longer needed there? We had not received any letters asking if we could return. The mission had been just super during this entire time of recovery. They made no demands and were very sensitive and supportive of our needs.

But what if, in fact, we were no longer needed in Ecuador? We were sensing in a new way God's call upon our lives and we were praying for God's clear guidance about our future service.

Just as the summer was ending, we prayed, "Lord, if we are to return to Quito, please have someone write and tell us that we are needed there." Shortly thereafter, we received a letter from the mission asking if we would be willing and able to coordinate the 50th Anniversary Celebration of HCJB. Talk about rejoicing! For the first time in four years, we really knew where we were headed. We never doubted that the Lord was in control, but the discipline of waiting had been a long and often discouraging learning experience.

It is clear to us that through it all the Lord brought those wilderness experiences into our lives for a purpose. He did not deal with us by a series of actions which were like punctuation marks in our lives, between which He moved off to deal with some other saint and then later returned His attention to us. His dealing with us was a process in which, although we could not always sense His presence, we knew that He was with us.

The best learning experiences were the hands-on experiences of practice. God allowed us to practice faith, trust, and patience daily. He even allowed us to make mistakes, but He was always there guiding us in our life's laboratory experience of living with Him. And while our Christian walk was like a laboratory science, He provided us with a perfect and infallible manual which, when we heeded it, made all our experiences successful. Sometimes our experiences had to be repeated to reinforce learning. We were again learning the leading of God in our lives.

Many of our friends in Portland prayed with us, and the little fellowship to which we belonged was quick to get behind us. While we were experiencing the joy of moving ahead under His direction, we faced another difficult separation from those whom we had come to love in Portland and the Northwest.

All during our time in the States, our personal friends remained faithful with us in prayer and financial support. Upon notice of our intention to return to the field, they pledged their continued backing for our ministry. It was amazing and confirming to have had their loving and faithful undergirding during this long period. They had persevered with us through it all, and now they were still a part of our lives and ministry. In eager anticipation of our return to South America, my mind slipped into high gear with ideas for HCJB's Golden Jubilee Celebration.

10

Back to Ecuador

The decision to leave Ecuador had been a difficult one. However, the decision to return was also fraught with various problems. Although I was thrilled to see the Lord leading us back to Quito, and into the meaningful ministry we had left four years before, I was also keenly aware that He was not just leading us back—He was leading us on.

Though the ministry of HCJB was basically the same, many other aspects of the Quito we once knew had changed. I would not occupy the same job I had when I left, many of our friends would not be there, and we would not live in the same apartment we once enjoyed so much. A year earlier, Lois and I had returned to Quito and sold most of our possessions, because it looked so doubtful that we would ever return. Thus, the furniture and other family artifacts which the children remembered were no longer there.

Tommy always looked back on Ecuador with great memories and often wished that we could return. He thought if he could be with all of his former friends, he wouldn't be lonely.

Now, faced with the opportunity, Tom began to realize that he was not the same person as when he left Quito years before, and that his friends would not be the same either. For four years their inner circle of relationships had been growing stronger and he had not been a part of that circle.

All of us wish at some time that we could go back to the way things were. Even when times are good we still have those moments in our lives when we wish we could relive some of those special times which included particularly meaningful experiences and people. Now the setting in which those events took place no longer exists and many of those special individuals have moved away or gone on to eternity.

But the times when we tend to look back are greater when we face difficult moments in our lives. When we are bereaved we want to return to the times when our loved one was with us. When we are sick or disabled, we want to go back to the days when we were well and able to function in ways that we can no longer.

But we can never go back. The backward look, though filled with many wonderful memories, can never lead us into a successful or meaningful future. Life is an ongoing proposition. He who only looks back begins to merely exist, not live. No matter what the past has been, the future will be different. But being different does not necessarily mean it will be worse. It can be much better. God has been good in the past and He has not changed. When we follow Him, He makes all of our tomorrows count for the best and the highest.

We would not go back. We would return to Quito and to HCJB, but we would go forward. Tom would not go back. He would return to the Alliance Academy and to many of the friends he had known in earlier days, but he would go forward.

During the last several months before our departure for Ecuador, Becky stayed with us in Oregon. It felt great having her in the family circle again. Her relationship with Tom had grown measurably. She took extra time to be with the younger children as well, and we all counted ourselves blessed by the added privilege of having her home again.

Since our plans were to leave Portland in the fall, we began to raise the support we needed before our return to the field. We planned to be in the Wheaton area for several weeks to get Becky settled in school before heading on south to Latin America. She had been accepted at Wheaton College and was planning to begin school in the winter quarter.

One of the neat ways the Lord confirmed our decision to return to the field took place on the day prior to leaving Portland. One of the concerns we had about returning to Ecuador was transportation. In all of the years of service prior to Tom's accident, we rode the public buses in Quito. Over the years, as the city began to outgrow the transportation system, the buses became more and more crowded, to the point where it was difficult to get on and off.

We often got shoved to the back of the bus, and since the aisles were always full of people, it was necessary to begin struggling forward well ahead of the desired stopping place. To do that required an excellent sense of balance, and that Tom did not have.

To be sure, he had come a long way. He had been included with the other students in his physical education classes at Aloha High School in Oregon. But in addition, he had his own program of exercise to carry out. When the students ran laps, Tom ran with them galloping as he went with his limp. Of course, they would all lap him several times. Many would pass along encouraging remarks to him as they whizzed by. Lois found a T-shirt with the picture of a turtle wearing a jogging suit and the inscription, "Slow but Steady." Tom wore this often and it became a sign of his growing self-acceptance. In spite of his physical improvement, he still lacked the athletic prowess needed to handle the Quito bus system.

We decided to trade our car, which had been given to us by the Faith Reformed Church in South Holland, Illinois several years earlier, on some sort of vehicle that could be shipped to Ecuador. A dear Japanese friend in Portland expressed great concern that we would get stuck with a lemon if we traded our car for a used one. The days passed and the time came for us to leave Portland. We found ourselves waist deep in barrels and crates. With only one day left before leaving, we still had too much to do. We had been working well past midnight for several days, trying to get everything ready for shipping.

On the next to last morning before our departure, I was scheduled to speak to a men's breakfast at the Mountain Park Church of Lake Oswego. This had been arranged by our friend, Tatsuya Ban. I remember so well arriving at the church at 6:00 A.M., thoroughly exhausted from the late nights we spent packing. I was so tired that I struggled with sleep during the entire meeting, even while I was speaking! I felt rather ashamed of my performance that morning and I hoped that they didn't get the idea that I was not enthused about our ministry at HCJB. The truth of the matter was that I was physically drained.

After I finished my remarks, Tatsuya stood up and said, "I would like you to pray about something. The Fulghums really need a van to take with them to Ecuador. I am concerned that when they trade their car, they might not get a good one, since they plan to buy a used one. Will you pray that they get a good car to take with them?"

With that announcement and a word of prayer, the meeting ended. As the men were leaving, one gentleman walked up to me and with a big smile on his face said, "I'd like to get you a van." For some reason I thought he was just expressing that he wished he could help us get one, so I responded with a glib,

"Sure, why not?" I laughed and thought we had both made rather good jokes. But he began to ask other questions which immediately let me know that he was not kidding. He really wanted to buy us a van! I quickly sprang from drowsiness into shock.

He left some instructions with several other men of the church and vanished. I never saw him again. I hurried home to tell Lois. Not much time passed before the phone rang and we were asked if we could be at the church at 1:30 that afternoon. We were instructed to bring our car and title papers. That same afternoon at 4:00, we drove off the lot with a new Ford van which would serve us well in Quito.

Deputation done and Becky in school, we left the States and returned to Ecuador. It had been almost four years to the day from the time that we had left. We all had many questions in our minds about the future, but we maintained our confidence that we were walking in the will of God, and that this was the most important thing of all.

Tom was quick to share his desire to do the will of God, and was always looking for a ministry of his own. He often came into our room at night and said, "Can we pray about my future? I really want to have the Lord's will for my life and right now I just don't know what He wants me to do." We sought to encourage him and answered, "Well, Tom, when the Lord is ready for you to know His will, He will see to it that you don't miss it."

All the children made good adjustments in their return to the Alliance Academy. The only area where they really struggled was in speaking Spanish, which they had all but forgotten. All, that is, except for Tom who, in spite of the damage his brain received, quickly jumped right into conversation with anyone who was interested in talking with him. And he did an amazingly good job of it.

He loved to converse with our maid, Olga, who had a deep and lasting love for him. She had cared for him when he was a small boy and had recognized his special quality of sensitivity toward others. While we were away, Tom occasionally wrote Olga letters or sent her a little offering to help meet the needs of her large family. We thought his generosity was an unusual quality for a boy his age. He was never selfish or unthoughtful, at least not when his thought processes were working well.

Tom's friends were genuinely glad to see him back in Ecuador again. They were quick to receive him, and at first invited him to all their social events. They tried to cope with his handicaps and the fact that he was less "with it" than they, since he had missed some of life's experiences in the outside world. But the invitations grew fewer and fewer until the only social life he had involved group activities or those which he initiated himself. With the exception of his involvement with the English Fellowship Church, which had a very active youth group, he was as alone as he had been in Oregon.

Tom threw himself into the youth group activities and became involved in the Christian Service Outreach group at the school. Even though he was rarely invited to join the small groups when they made weekend plans to go bowling, or out for pizza, or to someone's house for games, he gained a new and better acceptance of himself.

On one occasion a student said to him, "Tom, why don't you look at me with both eyes? I don't like the way one eye wanders when you talk to me." When relating the incident later that day, Tom said, "You know, he really needs prayer. He is in worse shape than I am." That demonstrated the great amount of growth that had taken place in Tom. No anger or resentment flared in what he said. His philosophical statement was absolutely correct.

Tom grew more independent in his studies as the year went

by. From the time of his release from the hospital, three and one-half years earlier, Lois had spent time every evening helping him with his homework. She literally gave herself to Tom as his tutor, confidant, and image builder. She was the family mediator where Tom was concerned, and rarely showed the impatience she must have felt from time to time.

She not only acted as Tom's defender, but also gave him counsel in a way that was not threatening to him. Even though he'd have a bad day at school, he knew he could come home and be comforted by Lois. I was much more impatient with him, and would often resort to sarcasm to correct Tom, especially when I felt he asked a question that had an obvious answer, or made a silly remark.

There were others who used sarcasm with him as well. One of Tom's teachers who cared about him very much used it frequently. She tried to get him to think for a minute before he made a statement or asked a needless question. Tom was convinced that the teacher did not like him. His friends also used sarcasm with him for the same reasons.

Some people use sarcasm when they can't handle situations they are facing. Rather than come out and say what they are really thinking or voice a frustration they are experiencing, they use sarcasm. People who do this are actually expressing their inability to cope, their lack of courage to face head-on the realities around them, or their inability to say what they really mean. While it may be a cowardly ploy to avoid honest communication, it's sometimes the easiest method to use.

Lois was the one who helped Tom keep his perspective on life and provided him with the greatest amount of genuine understanding. She was also the one who could talk with him most straightforwardly and helpfully about his problems.

During the first year after our return to Ecuador, Tom showed a growing ability to handle things for himself. He would come home and delve into his homework. It required more effort for him than for the average kid, but he had the self-discipline and the self-motivation to do it. Rarely did he need a major amount of help, and as the year progressed he came to the place where he could handle even the most difficult assignments by himself.

As Tom grew in his self-acceptance and his ability to handle his homework on his own, he also grew in his sense of responsibility. He actively participated in the band, the choir, Christian Service Outreach, and had different responsibilities in his class. Regardless of whether he felt important to the group or not, he could be counted on to be there and give his best for the cause.

The young people in his class accepted him as best they knew how. They were always friendly to him, and sometimes were protective as well. They supported his attempts at various activities, and he would try almost anything. I often said to him, "Tom, I'd rather you be handicapped physically and have the spirit which you have toward the Lord and toward others, than be a superstar and not have the qualities that really count." I don't know of any other place where Tom could have had better support from his friends and teachers than he had at the Alliance Academy. Tom grew to the place where he accepted his social isolation better than his mom or I did.

During the time that Tom progressed, I recovered from my mid-life crisis, and became thoroughly excited about my responsibilities at HCJB. In addition to my work as coordinator for the 50th Anniversary of HCJB, I accepted an invitation to serve as the Director of Communications. In my opinion, the ministry of HCJB had become more strategic and important than it was when I was Broadcast Director years before.

Lois experienced tremendous fulfillment doing what she felt called to—teaching missionary kids at the Alliance Academy.

The time of study during our long wait in the U.S. now served her and the students she taught well. Her Quito students enjoyed her as much as her Wheaton students had. And Tom and our other children loved having her at the school.

Academically, Tom continued to make good progress. Since he had only one functioning eye, reading was laborious for him. The subjects which required heavy reading assignments were consequently more difficult for him. But his grades were good and he even made the honors list a few times.

As his senior year passed and his friends busied themselves making college plans or applying for jobs in the U.S., Tom became concerned about his future. Several of his teachers believed he needed a year of growth before plunging into a college situation, and we tended to agree with them. Considering that we would be in a different hemisphere of the world, we were concerned about how he would do if he were entirely on his own.

Many of the missionary kids, who left the rather closed environment of a small mission school to enter into a larger and more impersonal world, had encountered numerous difficulties in making the necessary adjustments. Some who had not struggled with the odds that Tom faced had given up during their first year of college and returned home to try again the next year. For all these reasons, several individuals expressed concern at the thought of Tom stepping out into a world of independence and pressure.

But if Tom didn't go on to something else, what would he do at home? He needed the challenge of new experiences in order to continue his growth. It had been the challenge of school that had helped to bring him this far. We knew that there was little or no opportunity for meaningful work for Tom in Ecuador. He couldn't just go out and get a job in the Latin culture like he might in the U.S., and anyway, our visa would not allow it.

Even though the Academy offered to teach him a special program consisting of college level courses if Tom chose to remain out of college a year, we knew that one or two college courses would not be enough to keep him busy. Besides, all of his classmates would be gone, and his social development would be greatly reduced. His world would consist almost entirely of adults. In many ways Tom related to adults better than he did his peers, because of his association with nurses, doctors, therapists, educational specialists, and our friends. But we didn't want him to miss out on his youth. He had experienced some of the more serious aspects of living. We wanted him to have some fun.

But what if he could not be successful in college? Would he be able to handle the pressures of college life so far away from home? Where would he go? Who would he stay with? Would someone be interested enough in him to take him on as a son and give him a home away from home when he needed it? These were the questions which loomed in our minds.

For Tom, the question of the future was top priority. He was willing to stay with us for another year if that was what the Lord wanted. He wasn't in a hurry to get away from the family. But he had a sense of destiny for his own life. He felt that the Lord wanted him to continue to move ahead, not to vegetate and wait for another year to go by. He didn't want there to be a year's pause in his growth and development. He was ready to grow some more. He earnestly sought to know the will of God, ready to obey, no matter what it meant. He doubted that it meant staying out of school a year.

Upon recommendation from a psychologist who visited the school, Lois and I decided that in order to answer questions regarding Tom's academic potential, we needed to seek professional help and guidance. We believed he would probably be successful as far as the academics of college were concerned, but we wanted this confirmed. It was like following the biblical tradition of showing oneself to the priest to verify God's restoration and healing. We were hoping to verify God's restoring of Tom's brain to normal potential, through assessment by a qualified doctor.

Tom's senior year passed so swiftly. Almost before we knew it, the time had come for him to graduate. He reached this without any special favors and without lowering of the requirements. His diploma showed no deficiencies in his academic program. He attained that milestone with mostly A's and B's on his report card. That year his favorite Scripture was Philippians 4:13, "I can do all things through Christ who strengtheneth me." Christ had been his helper.

11
A Step to the Future

The cloudiness of that day in May could not dim the splendor of what Tom's graduation meant to all of us who loved him. It was doubly special for me because I had been asked to deliver the commencement address. I spent hours thinking about what I wanted to say to my son and the others who would be finishing one stage of life and beginning another. In addition to its meaning of graduation, commencement also signified a new beginning for the young people, and we hoped that it would be exactly that for Tom. The time had come for him to begin to live his own life, and we wanted that for him.

I looked into the faces of the graduates, all of whom held the highest expectations for their futures. Some would have great success in their tomorrows, but some would fail. Some would experience great blessing in their endeavors, but others would struggle. Some would face tragedies of life similar to those Tom had already known. Some would fulfill their parents' dreams for them and move on to successfully build their lives with Christ at the center, and establish Christian homes. Others would bring their parents pain and disappointment because of their future choices.

As with every graduating class, it was impossible to determine at the moment who would be in which category. But I prayed for all of them, that some word of counsel I would share would help someone make a wiser decision or avoid a pitfall in the future.

Some of these young people had grown up in the cloistered society of the Alliance Academy and the missionary community of Quito. When faced with the heat of the secular, pressure-cooker society outside, many would struggle arduously to maintain their sense of direction. It is not uncommon for MKs (missionary kids), who have lived most of their lives in such a warm and supportive environment, to have difficulty adjusting to being on their own.

But at this moment, the faces of the graduates revealed only a sense of achievement and expectancy for the very best. And in the midst of those bright and expectant faces was the smiling, hope-filled countenance of my son.

At times I struggled with the tear at the back of my voice that sought to insert itself in my speech as I gave the young people the proverbs of a father to his children. I knew that they were all hoping my address would be short and to the point so that they could get on with the more important matters of the day's agenda, the awarding of diplomas. I kept my remarks to 20 minutes and when the address ended, the moment for which they had waited began. It was the most significant moment for all of us. It was a moment which years earlier seemed to be an impossibility as far as our Tom was concerned.

"What should I do?" I wondered. "Should I stand up and applaud, or should I walk over and give him a big hug as he comes across the stage?"

"Thomas David Fulghum." The principal called his name as

he stepped onto the platform. The applause rose as with all the others before him, but it continued to rise as he limped across the stage.

"This is his moment," I mused, "and I mustn't get into it. He deserves to savor it all by himself."

It was a brief moment, but it was jammed full of struggles and dreams, hopes and accomplishments. Tom looked great in his cap and gown, and in the new suit he had received for the occasion. And while we rejoiced at the enormous achievement of the past, we acknowledged the continuing struggles of his future, a future that was still filled with many perplexing questions.

For months Tom's real desire had been to go away to school, like many of his classmates. In most ways, we wanted that for him, but questions had been raised about what his success might be if he did.

Several months earlier we met with a number of his teachers and the school counselor, all of whom wondered if it might be better for Tom to remain at home for another year. They had worked with him in his classes and, while he did quite well academically, he was still behind his classmates socially.

"Perhaps another year of growth will allow him to catch up in some important areas before jumping into the college world," they remarked. They felt he was still too dependent upon others. They wanted to maximize the possibilities for his success and minimize the chances for failure.

As his parents, we had some of the same concerns. He was still dependent in many areas at home as well and, although he had made a great deal of progress during that year, it was difficult to imagine how he would do in a dormitory situation.

"But what will I do if I stay here?" he asked. "There isn't an opportunity for a job, and all of my friends will be gone. I feel I'd just be wasting a whole year and I don't want to spend time doing nothing. I need to be challenged with something. I need to grow, not vegetate."

He was right. We discussed the pros and cons of staying home or going on to school during the weeks and months just prior to graduation. Frequently, during the days just before commencement, Tom came into our bedroom in the evening with questions or ideas concerning his future. But as the time for graduation neared, and his frustration over the matter grew, we knew we'd have to make a decision.

Lois and I were scheduled to make a trip to the U.S. as a part of HCJB's 50th anniversary celebration. We would be in Chicago for one month, and decided to take Tom with us. One evening, when Tom came into our room concerned about why the Lord had not given us clear guidance about what he was to do the next year, I said to him, "Tom, Mom and I are going to take you with us to the States when we go in July. It will be a venture of faith for all of us, and you'll have a chance to see the Lord lead you very specifically as far as your future is concerned. We'll look at several schools as we travel, and have some testing done on your ability to do college work. When we get to the place where the Lord wants you to be, He will make that perfectly clear."

Lois and I had often seen the Lord guide in marvelous and amazing ways in our own lives, and we had shared some of those experiences with our children. To every young person who grows up in a Christian home, the moment comes to experience that same kind of leading for himself. Tom definitely had a close and personal relationship with the Lord. This would be a special opportunity to experience the Lord's direct leading for himself.

We left Quito in late June and flew to Miami. There we picked up the car that would be our transportation during the month we would be in the U.S. The first stop in our pilgrimage was the Miami Bible College, near HCJB's International Office. We wondered if this would be the best place for Tom since it was near the HCJB headquarters, and closer to Quito than other schools. I could see Tom once in a while since I passed through Miami three or four times a year on business trips.

When we visited the school, the summer staff were present, and they were kind, understanding, and positive people. Tom rather liked the school, but we had decided that we would look at several possibilities, and when he saw the right one he would know it, for the Lord would give him a perfect peace about it.

Tom applied to the Moody Bible Institute in Chicago prior to graduation, but when they received his references, they indicated that it might be good for Tom to wait a year before entering the school. They recommended he advise them the following spring if he was still interested in attending there.

Since our HCJB assignment would lead us through Indianapolis on our way to Chicago, we decided to stop and visit Lois' mother, and her sister and family who had moved there very recently. It was great to see them in a new environment and well settled with exciting responsibilities.

"We thought that Tom would like to stay with us," they offered.

"You mean, Tom can stay here while we complete our special assignment in Chicago?" we asked.

"Well, that would be all right too, but we thought Tom would like to live with us this next year and go to school in Indianapolis. After we moved here, we found a little Baptist college just a mile or so from our house. Perhaps you'd like to take a look at it."

We had never heard of Indiana Baptist College. But since we had decided to make an earnest search for God's guidance, we agreed to visit the school the very next day.

Indiana Baptist College is a small school operated by a church.

It is unaccredited and offers majors in Bible, Christian Education, Music, and Education. The staff was courteous, open, and encouraging concerning Tom. With only 120 students enrolled, it would provide the kind of environment where Tom could develop. He liked the school and later that afternoon when we returned to his cousin's home, announced that he thought he wanted to attend there.

"Before you make a final decision," I cautioned, "there are some things about the school I think you should understand. The school has regulations that you must support if you decide to attend there. Let me read them for you."

As I began to read the school's standard of conduct and requirements, Tom's face fell. His hair would have to be off his collar with his ears visible from every direction. He would have to wear a shirt and tie to classes each day, and a suit on certain social occasions. As far as relationships with the opposite sex was concerned, the six-inch rule applied; and when riding in a car, the distance between girls and guys increased to two feet. All music would have to be approved by a committee, and attendance at various kinds of amusements was strictly forbidden.

Many of these items posed no problem for Tom, but he rather enjoyed having his hair over his ears, and he was not prone to dress up to go to school. The music rule might also be a problem for him, although he was not a rock music buff.

When I finished reading the list, Tom went upstairs without speaking. He returned shortly with a smile on his face, and announced, "Well, I just prayed about it and feel this is the school where the Lord wants me to go. I like the school. I can live with the rules without any problem, and I would be happy staying with Aunt Ellie, Uncle Lloyd, Cliff, and Grandma.

It was obvious that he was pleased. And Lois and I were so happy about his decision that we all knew the Lord had arranged the whole thing. Tom would be in a small school with a good program and a supportive staff, and in the home of family who loved him. We could never have planned anything better for him.

12
Tough
Love

There were still a few questions that needed answers before we could enroll Tom in a college. The main items to be taken care of were the testing and evaluations by the doctors and the psychologist. We drove on to Wheaton and quickly made the necessary arrangements.

We took Tom back to the Marianjoy Rehabilitation Hospital to have an evaluation made by Dr. Pesch, who had cared for Tom five years earlier. He entered the office smiling, with Tom's records under his arm.

"Well, Tom, how nice to see you again, and looking so good!" He was a kindly man, able to express honestly what he believed about a patient without being threatening or aloof. "Well, let's have a look at you and see how you are doing."

He began testing Tom's reflexes, doing strength tests, and checking such things as balance and perception. He referred to Tom's records from time to time. "Oh, that's come back! That's great!" he exclaimed every once in awhile, obviously pleased. After several different examinations, he said, "Tom, you are stronger than I am. You've done very well. Your walk is a little sloppy though. You don't have to bob and weave all over the place like that." Lois chuckled out loud. That was exactly what she had been telling him.

"Pretend you have a line fastened to the top of your head," he gestured with his hand, "which is pulling you straight and tall and keeping you from moving from side to side." Lois chuckled even more loudly because this too was what she had been telling him. Tom grinned back at her.,

"Well, Tom, you're doing just great. I don't think there's anything more to be done."

That was reassuring to us and affirming to Tom. We took a walk through the hospital. Each area we entered was filled with memories of much more difficult days. We saw many other people who were in the throes of their own trials, walking in the ways that we had walked before them.

The next visit was to the psychologist. The whole idea bothered Tom, as he didn't like the prospect of going to a "shrink." We assured him that he was going to a doctor who could help us understand both his abilities and aptitudes, as well as his weaknesses. He would give us better insight into planning his future in ways that would maximize his opportunities for success and minimize the chances of failure.

With that explanation, Tom was satisfied. He was even more pleased when he met Dr. Hocking. He found him to be sympathetic and positive. He was a good conversationalist, but he was also a very good listener.

Often Lois and I had wondered if we were perhaps the ones who needed the help of a psychologist. We had kept a certain steady pressure on Tom to continue his improvement. At times we wondered if the pressure had been too great and had done more harm than good. Had we encouraged him enough or had we been more of a discouragement to him than a help? Our intentions had always been the best, but often our approach seemed sadly lacking. Would some of our failures be reflected in Tom's psyche? These questions were always in our minds. The whole thing was a little scary.

Tom spent five hours with the doctor on three different occasions, after which an evaluation period was scheduled for the following Friday. We arrived early for our appointment and were all a bit apprehensive about what the evaluation might reveal. What might his recommendations be for Tom? For us? Could Tom expect to be successful if he returned to that little school in Indianapolis? Would this testing be sufficient, or would he recommend some further course of action? Who really needed more help—Tom, or Lois and I?

Dr. Hocking walked into the reception room smiling, especially greeted Tom, and invited us all to join him in his office. It was decorated more like a sitting room than an office, with a small table in the center and comfortable chairs around the room. Attractive warm pictures hung on the walls and the atmosphere was relaxed and friendly. Coffee was on the table and he invited us to join him for a cup.

"You have a very special son!" he said as he sat down. "I have enjoyed every minute of the time I have spent with him."

"We know that," we agreed. "We have known that since he was very small." Tom listened smiling, gratified by the expressions of praise.

"Let me explain what we've been doing during the long sessions we have spent together. We've been trying to get some insights into Tom's attitudes and feelings toward himself, others, life, and his future. The tests we gave him have helped us get a glimpse of what is going on in his mind."

We nodded eagerly. These were the things we wanted to know.

"Plus," he continued, "we worked to get a handle on what

his potential is for the future." We especially wanted to hear about that.

"We gave Tom three basic tests. The first shows his perceptual skills and powers of concentration. I showed him various geometric designs for varying lengths of time and asked him to reproduce them as best he perceived and remembered them. The length of time he was given to view and reproduce these designs varied with the complexity of the designs to be remembered."

He pulled a folder off a nearby table and placed the original designs and Tom's reproductions on the center of the table in front of us. My eyes widened as I looked at the beautiful drawings Tom had made. They were almost all identical in shape, proportion, and size to the originals. Only in a few cases were there differences. Dr. Hocking was obviously very pleased. So was Tom, and so were we. The results were especially significant to Tom, because he, like the rest of us, had been concerned about his retentive powers. My eyes moistened with tears of gratitude to the Lord who had done so much for Tom.

"The second test deals with Tom's views of himself, life, his future, and his home. I asked Tom to draw certain things for me to get an idea of how he views various aspects of life. First of all, I asked him to draw a picture of a boy, and this is what he drew."

He laid an excellent drawing on the table of a boy with his hands in his pockets. The boy had his left leg propped up on a large log lying in front of him. The drawing was terrific. Lois studied the sketch with a puzzled look on her face. She had the feeling that she had seen the picture somewhere before.

"In the first place, Tom, I suggest that you have drawn a picture of yourself. Here is the picture of a boy who is smiling, healthy looking, and who in every way seems to have a good feeling about his life. There is an air of confidence in this picture. I believe that Tom has a similar feeling about himself. He is hopeful, confident, and has a good self-esteem and ego. There is only one thing about the picture that tells us something different. Do you notice anything that suggests to you what that might be?"

We all stared at the drawing as he spoke, interested by what he had to say. "Do you mean the fact that the boy has his left leg on the log?" Lois asked.

"Yes," he replied. "Exactly! The left leg propped up may indicate that Tom has some sensitive feelings about his own short left leg."

Suddenly Lois began rummaging through her purse and pulled out an envelope from which she produced a picture of our second son, Brian. "I knew I had seen that picture before. Tom, were you thinking about this picture of Brian when you drew your picture?"

"Phoooey" Tom muttered. "I thought his hands were in his pockets."

In the photo Brian had his hands on his hips, but other than that the picture was an excellent rendition.

"Well," the doctor laughed, "for a boy who is supposed to have such a poor memory, you have recalled this very well. And though this is not a picture of yourself, it still shows a strong and healthy outlook on life. That view shows up in many other areas of the testing as well. For example," he spoke to Lois and me again, "I asked Tom to draw a picture of a tree, and this is what he drew."

He placed the second drawing on the table. It depicted a massive tree with an enormous trunk. There were little flowers growing around the base, and some of the roots which extended outward had been bared by the passing of time. The branches were laden with foliage.

"This tree is a strong, friendly, old tree which is loaded with life," the doctor stated. "It isn't just any old tree. It is a tree that has character and gives a feeling of strength, stability, and permanence. It's a tree that provides others with beauty. It is, though an old tree, a soft tree and the little flowers around it add to its friendly beauty. It's the kind of tree that you would want to have a picnic under, isn't it?"

We all agreed that it was. All of what he had said was true of that tree. It was a tremendous drawing, and it gave us all those feelings of strength, friendliness, and stability.

"The third drawing that I asked Tom to make was of a house. This is his drawing." Tom's drawing showed a three dimensional house of beautiful proportions. There were windows all across the second floor of the house. It was well constructed, neat, and cheerful.

"Tom told me about this house and some of the things which go on there. It is a family home. That second floor with all the windows is the game room where most of the family activities take place."

Tom smiled his approval at Dr. Hocking's description of his drawing, indicating his concurrence with his evaluation of it too.

"He has a very happy feeling about his home and about his family. He loves you all very much. This too has come out in numerous ways during our times together."

By this time it was difficult to control the tears which sought to reveal the emotions we were feeling. "Sometimes we were afraid that through all of this, we might have pushed him too hard, or made things more difficult for him. There were times when we corrected him so often and tried so hard to make him like everyone else that we were afraid we might have damaged his self-image, or even pushed him to the point of resentment."

"Tom," Dr. Hocking smiled thoughtfully, "you have been the recipient of what I call 'tough love.' "

"My parents have been great," Tom said enthusiastically. "They were the ones who encouraged me and always helped me keep moving ahead in my improvement.

By this time we were crying. Crying for the love of our son. Crying with gratitude to the Lord for the "tough love" He had given to all of us, to see us through the deep waters together. We were crying with gratitude that we had come through it all with our family not only intact, but stronger than when we entered.

"The third test we gave Tom indicates his potential for the future."

We all sat up because we wanted to know what to expect for Tom's development. We needed to know how to plan, and since Lois and I would be returning to Ecuador in a matter of days, we needed to know right away.

"The tests show that Tom is socially about a year behind other young people his age in what I call life's experiences."

This was no news to us. He missed the better part of a year during the times he was hospitalized and his mind was so turned in on itself. He remembered very little of what went on during that entire year.

"But," the doctor continued, "the test shows that he has plenty of ability in the areas which are necessary for him to be successful in college."

Tom beamed pure joy on hearing that statement. He was so pleased that it seemed he grew taller in his chair as we went over each of the tests.

"Tom has the ability to reason in the abstract, and in particular, has a strong capacity in language arts. He has plenty of ability to conceptualize, and his perception and memory are all above average. He can remember precisely the things he wants to remember."

Lois grinned at that one, because whenever Tom really wanted to do something, you couldn't make him forget it.

"He needs to improve in the area of concentration and, as I said, he is a little short in life experiences, but that will come. In all the areas that really count, he has abilities which are at least average and in many areas well above. Tom, you have every reason to expect to be successful in college if you apply yourself to it. And as far as I can see, you can be anything you really want."

Our thoughts raced back over the years, the dismal pronouncements by some of the doctors, and Tom's battles and struggles. But we also remembered the progress, the victories, and especially the promises that at times seemed to be unattainable, but which were always moorings to which we could tie our hopes. Especially that early promise from Psalm 91—"I will satisfy him with a full life and give him My salvation."

There was an extra lilt in Tom's limp and in his voice as we left the clinic that afternoon. It was as if he had stepped out of the shadows and into the brightness of his future. We could make arrangements for him to go to the little school in Indianapolis with confidence. And he had the assurance of his own potential as well.

One of the last things he said before we left the clinic was, "Well, I'm going out to seek my fortune." We all laughed at his purposeful declaration, but we knew that in a real sense it was true. He was ready to enter the world on his own. He had what it would take for him to accomplish his goals, serve the Lord, and be a blessing to others by making a contribution to those around him.

Of course, the last chapters of Tom's story are being kept in heaven waiting to be revealed, as are the chapters of all of our lives. But the God who keeps those precious pages in the hollow of His hand is the One who loves us. And whether His love is gentle or tough, it is eternal.